A SHORT HISTORY

by

A. A. McALISTER

of H. Hogarth & Sons Limited

and

FLEET LIST

by

LEONARD GRAY

of World Ship Society

Published by The World Ship Society
Kendal LA9 7LT
1976

Goodwin & Hogarth, Ship Chandlers and Sailmakers, Winton Buildings, Dock Road, Ardrossan

Photographed circa. 1870

2

A SHORT HISTORY

The early years of the nineteenth century saw the development of Ardrossan, Ayrshire, as a port of increasing importance, when it gradually superceded its neighbour, Saltcoats, in the role as the most important port along that part of the Ayrshire coast.

The development of a port inevitably means that within its boundaries there become established businesses and organisations having a direct link with ships and the sea and Ardrossan was no exception in this respect. When a port is endeavouring to attract trade it must be able to provide all the ancillary services and one of these essential shipping services is that of Shipchandler. It is at this juncture that the name of Hogarth assumes some prominence in shipping circles in Ardrossan and, before many years had passed, this prominence had extended well beyond the bounds of the town of Ardrossan and the County of Ayr.

The man largely responsible for this increasing prominence was Hugh Hogarth, who was born at Stevenston, Ayrshire, in 1840, the youngest child of the family of six — five sons and one daughter — of Robert and Ann Hogarth of that town. Robert Hogarth was the son of John Hogarth, a sailor of Stevenston, born on 22nd November, 1794.

In 1862 Hugh Hogarth joined Captain James Goodwin to form a business as Ship Store Merchants, trading in Ardrossan under the name of Goodwin and Hogarth. Captain Goodwin was a Galloway man who started his working life as a sailor before the mast and subsequently rose to command. From the start the business prospered and a sizeable part of this business was with Canadian shipping interests. This resulted in the development of a particular interest in trade with Eastern Canada and before many years had passed the two men decided to widen the scope of their activities by embarking on the business of Shipowning.

The first vessels acquired were wooden sailing ships, some built in yards in the Maritime Provinces of Canada — a part of the world which, at that time, enjoyed a high reputation for the standard of ship built, and which they employed mainly in the North Atlantic trade. Unfortunately, records establishing the precise dates of purchase of these ships and the order in which they were acquired are incomplete but it would appear that the first ship bought was the FEARLESS, a square-sterned, wooden brigantine with one deck and two masts of 238.60 gross tons, measuring 111' x 26.9' x 12.4', built in 1861 by Granville of Annapolis, Nova Scotia, and purchased on 29th August, 1868. She appears to have been followed by the DUKE OF WELLINGTON, a square-sterned barque with two decks and three masts of 468.34 gross tons built in Dumbarton and acquired on 22nd November, 1869. Neither ship was destined to trade for long under Goodwin and Hogarth's ownership for the FEARLESS was lost off Beachy Head in December, 1870 and the DUKE OF WELLINGTON met her end at St. Thomas, British West Indies, in August, 1870.

By this time, however, other ships had joined the fleet and reference to the accompanying Ship Histories will provide details. The aforementioned doubt and speculation expressed concerning which ship was in fact the first owned by Goodwin and Hogarth is heightened by the knowledge of the existence of a sailing vessel named VIRGINIE, listed in certain old records as owned by 'Hogarth of Ardrossan'. It would seem possible, however, that this ship might at one time have been owned by John Hogarth, Hugh Hogarth's eldest brother, who was born at Stevenston in 1822, the eldest of the family, but in view of the air of uncertainty which surrounds this ship she has not been included in the Ship Histories. If John Hogarth did indeed own the VIRGINIE, this seems to have been the only direct connection he had with shipowning as far as we know, apart from an interest in the sailing vessel KATE, another wooden ship, of 154 tons nett and built in 1852 in New Brunswick, possibly owned by him although she was managed by Goodwin and Hogarth.

It is worth recording here that, bearing in mind his close relationship to Hugh Hogarth and being eighteen years his senior, John Hogarth quite possibly had a strong influence over Hugh Hogarth during the latter's younger years. John Hogarth, too, rose to a position of considerable eminence in Ardrossan and the surrounding district. He owned a large ironmongery business, which he had founded, in the town and it can be said that for many years most of the large contracts for plumbing and slating work in the area were executed by the firm of J. Hogarth and Company. He entered the Ardrossan Town Council in 1851 and continued in office until 1893 when he retired, having given forty-two years service to the Council — for a number of them as Burgh Treasurer and for eleven as Chief Magistrate. He died on 29th May, 1898.

During the 1860's and 1870's the Goodwin and Hogarth fleet gradually expanded until it included the following sailing vessels: BRISK, BURNBRAE, EMMA L. OULTON, G. A. COONAN, JANE YOUNG, JESSIE GOODWIN, JOSEPHINE, KATE (already mentioned), MARY HOGARTH, MYSTIC TIE and DRUMADOON. It is possible that the JESSIE GOODWIN may have been built for Goodwin and Hogarth but more likely that she was bought from another owner and renamed. If the latter was the case, then in all probability the first ship which was actually built to their order was the MARY HOGARTH, a wooden barque of 588 nett tons, built in 1875 in New Brunswick.

Hugh Hogarth (Snr.) 1840-1904

The partnership remained in being, as accurately as can be assessed, until 1878, although the precise date of separation is uncertain owing to the lack of written records, but the vessel BURNBRAE may give some clue for in March, 1875 Hugh Hogarth ceased to have an interest in that ship although James Goodwin retained an interest in her until her loss in January, 1878. Although somewhat vague, it would therefore appear that the two men may have started to go their own separate ways prior to 1878. When the partnership ceased, Captain Goodwin kept the JESSIE GOODWIN, purchased the wooden barque TREVANION built in 1869, from Barrass and Company of London and had built to his order the three-masted schooner SIR HERBERT MAXWELL. She was of 231 tons and her builder was Barr of Ardrossan. Captain Goodwin did not live long after the cessation of the partnership for he died at Ardrossan in June, 1879.

Hugh Hogarth retained the G. A. COONAN, JOSEPHINE, MARY HOGARTH and DRUMADOON (the other vessels mentioned above had either been disposed of or lost prior to 1878) and acquired the wooden barques CYPRUS, built to his order in 1878 by Warlow of Milford Haven, and MODERN, built in 1877 in Quebec.

Although he continued to reside in Ardrossan — at 8 South Crescent — Hugh Hogarth moved his shipowning business to Glasgow in 1880, although here again the precise date cannot be ascertained, where he opened an office at 70 Great Clyde Street. At the same time he expanded his fleet of ships and in 1881 placed an order with Turnbull, of Whitby, for his first steamship. She was christened BARON ARDROSSAN and, as well as being the first of six ships to bear this name, she was the first Hogarth vessel to have the prefix 'Baron' which has been continued with every ship in the fleet since, and always the names of Scottish barons. It should also be mentioned at this juncture that every ship in the fleet, past and present, has been registered at Ardrossan, thus in a very real way perpetuating the link between the company and the port in which it had its origins.

Reference to the Ship Histories will provide information concerning all the additions to and departures from the fleet, but it is worth recording here that orders continued to be placed for sailing vessels and in 1883 Robert Duncan of Port Glasgow built for Hugh Hogarth the first of several handsome iron, full-rigged vessels which became well known in the ports of the world. This first full-rigged ship was the MACHRIHANISH, which gained a considerable reputation by proving herself a swift sailer. In his book *The Last of the Windjammers,* Basil Lubbock described her as "A beauty and the clipper of Hugh Hogarth's fleet". This enviable reputation resulted from several record passages which stand to her credit and perhaps the most notable of these was when, under the command of Captain J. A. Sanders, a Nova Scotian, she sailed from Portland, Oregon, with a full cargo of tinned salmon and, after crossing the Astoria Bar at the mouth of the Columbia River on 6th January, 1892, she arrived off Fastnet on 5th April, 1892 — eighty-nine days out. Another of her noteworthy passages was a ballast run from Cape Town to Otago

s.v. MACHRIHANISH

Heads, New Zealand, in thirty days, a feature of this run being that she and the New Zealand Shipping Company's s.s. PAPAROA left Table Bay together and both arrived off the New Zealand coast when twenty-six days out. The MACHRIHANISH was followed by OCHTERTYRE, CORRYVRECHAN, ARDNAMURCHAN, BALLACHULISH and COLINTRAIVE, but none of these proved as fast as MACHRIHANISH. The COLINTRAIVE was the last sailing vessel to be built for Hugh Hogarth and she had a tragically short life, being lost without trace in 1894, when only two years old, whilst on passage from Newcastle, N.S.W. to San Francisco with a cargo of coal. The last sailing ship to be owned by H. Hogarth and Sons (as the company was by then known) was the OCHTERTYRE, sold in 1910 to Norwegian buyers. To anyone not conversant with some of the place-names to be found in the West of Scotland, it is not difficult to appreciate why these sailing ships became known as the 'Hogarth Jawbreakers'!

An important change in the structure of the company took place on the 1st November, 1898 when Hugh Hogarth consolidated the ownership of a number of his ships by the formation of Hogarth Shipping Company Limited, of which Company he was appointed Manager. The five sailing vessels in the fleet at that time were, with BARON HUNTLY — a steel screw steamer built by Rodger, Port Glasgow, in 1895 — retained by

Hugh Hogarth while all the remaining steamers (the number of which had continued to increase since the building of BARON ARDROSSAN (1)) were taken over by Hogarth Shipping Company Limited. BARON HUNTLY differed from the other steamers in the fleet insofar that she had been built specifically for the Glasgow/Lisbon/Glasgow Berth Service and until quite recently the Company maintained an active interest in this trade although after 1963 none of the ships of the fleet had been employed on the Berth Service. The port of Huelva, in southern Spain, also received regular visits from 'Baron' vessels operating on the Berth Service — great quantities of pyrites ore mined by The Tharsis Sulphur and Copper Company Limited being shipped out of the port — and it is interesting to recall that during the Second World War one of the Company's masters, Captain Lachlan McPhail who was commanding BARON FORBES (1), attended the funeral at Huelva of 'the Man Who Never Was', the central figure in a carefully staged episode which might well have confused the Germans into thinking that the Allies would not land in Sicily.

It should also be mentioned that, as well as conducting the affairs of the Berth Service over the years, the office department which handled these matters also ran, and continues to run, the Agency Department, representing many owners whose ships call at Glasgow and the Clyde area.

A further change occurred in 1901 when Hugh Hogarth assumed as Partners his two elder sons, Samuel Crawford Hogarth, born in 1874, and Hugh Hogarth (Junior), born in 1876. At the same time the Firm's name was altered to H. Hogarth and Sons. Then, in 1903, a further company was formed — Kelvin Shipping Company Limited, with H. Hogarth and Sons acting as Managers, and this new Company took over BARON HUNTLY from H. Hogarth and Sons. This arrangement continued until 24th April 1904 when Hugh Hogarth, Senior, died suddenly whilst attending church service in Ardrossan, thus closing a chapter in the life of the Company. Although not ambitious of public life, Hugh Hogarth rose to a position of considerable eminence during his lifetime through constant effort and example. He had always maintained a real interest in the Ardrossan area and was particularly accessible and ready to give help and advice on seafaring matters. In June, 1876 he was elected the first Secretary of the Ayrshire Shipowners' Association; was Chairman of the Clyde Underwriting and Freight Demurrage Association, having been unanimously elected to that position on 11th March, 1892; was a Director of the Lanarkshire and Ayrshire Railway Company and of the Ardrossan Harbour Board. He was a Justice of the Peace for the County of Ayr and in 1903 was appointed Chairman of the North of England Protecting and Indemnity Association (in succession to Sir Robert Ropner, M.P.) and at the time of his death was Vice-President of the Glasgow Shipowners' and Shipbrokers' Benevolent Association.

On his father's death, S. Crawford Hogarth succeeded to the position of Senior Partner at the age of thirty. Under his guidance the fleet of steamers steadily expanded and the sailing vessels were gradually disposed of, the last finally going, as already mentioned, in 1910. In that year, too, Hugh Hogarth and Sons ceased to own ships in their own name, the fleet being divided between Hogarth Shipping Company Limited and Kelvin Shipping Company Limited. By this time, of course, the general tramping activities were, and had been for many years, world-wide and have remained so ever since — there can be few ports of the world which have not at some time acted as host to a 'Baron' ship.

At the outbreak of the First World War in August, 1914 the associated Companies owned between them twenty-three ships and, in common with other British shipping companies of that period, suffered severely from enemy action, fourteen vessels being lost. During the War a further three were sold and seven added to the fleet, resulting in the fleet consisting of thirteen ships on the termination of hostilities.

In 1919 Barclay Hogarth, the Founder's youngest son who was born in 1888, returned from active war service with the British Army and, together with John Baird Henderson, born in 1872 and who had been associated with the firm for many years, were assumed as Partners of H. Hogarth and Sons. John B. Henderson retired in 1936 and Barclay Hogarth died suddenly in 1951.

Also in the year 1919 the Company opened offices in London under the name of Hogarth Sons and Company Limited and the main function of this part of the Organisation was to carry out practically all the chartering of the ships of the fleet, as well as a considerable amount of chartering on behalf of foreign owners, which was in addition to chartering on behalf of The Tharsis Sulphur and Copper Company Limited.

It was during the early years of this century that the Company's offices were moved from 70 Great Clyde Street, to 24 St. Enoch Square, Glasgow, and in 1927 a move was made to 120 St. Vincent Street, Glasgow.

A few years prior to this last move, 1924, saw the formation of another Company, Iberia Shipping Company Limited, with H. Hogarth and Sons appointed as Managers. During its period of ownership of ships Iberia Shipping Company Limited owned three vessels — BARON FORBES (1), acquired in 1924 and perhaps one of the best-known vessels ever owned by the Organisation (and already mentioned in the reference to Huelva); BARON SALTOUN, acquired in 1927 and lost through enemy action in 1943; and BARON RAMSAY, built in 1929 and sold for breaking-up in 1959. In 1952 the name Iberia Shipping Company Limited was changed to H. Hogarth and Sons Limited.

During the 1920's and 1930's a continuous policy was operated of building new tonnage whilst disposing of older vessels when they ceased to be economic to run. This resulted in a steady increase in the total tonnage of the fleet and ensured the maintenance of efficiency and as a consequence, at the outbreak of the Second World War in September, 1939, the fleet consisted of thirty-nine ships, making it one of the largest, if not the largest, privately-owned tramping fleets in the world. Reference to the Ship Histories will reveal the types and classes of ship joining the fleet during this time and it should be recorded that, in spite of the depression and slump in the late '20s and early '30s, the Company was one of the very few in the United Kingdom which did not lay a ship up but, in fact, continued with a building programme.

S. Crawford Hogarth 1874-1950

It was during the late 1920's and into the 1930's that a Berth Service was maintained, in conjunction with Isbrandtsen Lines of New York, between that port and South African ports when regular sailings of 'Baron' ships meant the movement of large quantities of general and bulk cargoes to South Africa from the East Coast of the United States.

In 1935 Hugh Hogarth, born in 1909, the older son of S. Crawford Hogarth, was assumed a Partner of H. Hogarth and Sons and Alastair Crawford Hogarth, born in 1911, S. Crawford Hogarth's younger son, became a Partner of that Company in 1937.

The Second World War started in September, 1939 and during the next five years the fleet and the sea-going personnel suffered severely as a result of enemy action. As already mentioned, there were thirty-nine ships in the fleet in September, 1939 and a further two, the BARON SCOTT and the BARON HERRIES, were added the following year. By 1945 no fewer than twenty ships of the fleet had been lost and the Fleet List mentions the casualties. It can probably be said that the Second World War made even greater demands upon the ships and personnel of the Company than did the First. All the ships were taken over, from an operational point of view, by the Government, meaning that chartering activities ceased, so that at the cessation of hostilities in 1945 it was necessary to re-establish chartering relationships.

The Company's operations during the Second World War were not confined to 'Baron' ships for, in addition, H. Hogarth and Sons managed no fewer than thirty-six ships on behalf of the Ministry of War Transport, these being listed in the Ship Histories. Of these, twenty-six were, in the main, manned by British crews and the remaining ten carried crews of the owners' nationality. Of the twenty-six, seven were lost through enemy action and of the ten, six were casualties. Casualties suffered by British personnel sailing on 'Baron' and Ministry ships totalled no fewer than 324 killed and 42 wounded, a ratio which underlines the dangers which were faced by the Merchant Navy during the Wars. There were several awards for bravery made to sea-going personnel of the Company and the skill and fortitude displayed by so many of them is illustrated by part of the crew of BARON JEDBURGH (II) who, after their ship was torpedoed in the South Atlantic in March, 1945, succeeded in reaching the Brazilian coast in one of the ship's lifeboats under the command of the Master, Captain Eric A. Brown, after a voyage under sail of nearly two weeks. The remainder of the crew were rescued by a ship of the Union Castle Line shortly after their vessel foundered. As the total casualties for the fleet show, it is a sad fact that not all the sinkings resulting from enemy action had such a happy ending. At the close of hostilities in 1945 the ships remaining in the fleet numbered twenty-one.

In 1947 George Shand Brown, born in 1899, was assumed as a Partner of H. Hogarth and Sons, as was John MacKinlay MacLeod (born 1903), in 1952. The latter, on returning in 1945 from active service with the Royal Navy during the War, was placed in charge of the London Office, Hogarth Sons and Company Limited, and in that year, together with Ernest Stafford Tweedale (born 1906), was appointed a Director of that Company. Mr MacLeod retired from active business in 1967 and Mr Tweedale in 1966. Mr Brown also retired from active business in 1967 but both he and Mr MacLeod remain Directors of Hogarth Shipping Company Limited, H. Hogarth and Sons Limited and Hogarth Sons and Company Limited.

In 1952 the management of Hogarth Shipping Company Limited and Kelvin Shipping Company Limited was transferred from H. Hogarth and Sons to H. Hogarth and Sons Limited (formerly Iberia Shipping Company Limited) but this purely internal rearrangement did not in any way affect the continuity of management since the original Directors of H. Hogarth and Sons Limited, namely Hugh Hogarth, Alastair C. Hogarth, George S. Brown and John M. MacLeod, were the four persons who comprised the Partnership of H. Hogarth and Sons.

At the end of the Second World War five Ministry-owned ships which had been built during the War and managed by H. Hogarth and Sons were purchased — the BARON AILSA, BARON ELCHO, BARON ELIBANK, BARON GEDDES and BARON MURRAY and those 'Barons' which had survived the War were systematically put through survey, overhauled and returned to peace-time commercial service with many more years of useful trading life left in them. At this time some were converted from coal- to oil-fired boilers.

In 1950 S. Crawford Hogarth died and, although he had been in failing health for some time, he maintained a lively interest in the Company's activities until the end. Like his father, he had not sought publicity but, by example, hard work and endeavour he had built up a fine reputation and it was his foresight and ability which were in large measure responsible for the eminent position held by the firm in world shipping circles. In addition to his close association with the Company, he was a Director of Tharsis Sulphur and Copper Company Limited, The North of England Protecting and Indemnity Association Limited, the British Corporation (prior to its incorporation into Lloyds Register of Shipping) and the Bank of Scotland. As early as November, 1916 he had been elected to the Incorporation of Coopers of the Trades House of Glasgow and in October, 1926 he became a Freeman of the City of London.

The Company suffered a further death, in addition to Barclay Hogarth who died in 1951 as already mentioned, when Hugh Hogarth, the Founder's second son, died in 1954. He had retired from active participation in the affairs of the Firm in 1919.

In 1953 a new venture for the Comany commenced with the completion and commissioning at Caledon's Dundee Yard of the 16,500 deadweight tons bulk oil tanker BARON KILMARNOCK, unique in the history of the Organisation by being jointly owned by Hogarth Shipping Company Limited and Kelvin Shipping Company Limited. She was the first post-war 'Baron' to be built but she was closely followed by a class of six 9,500 deadweight tons 'tween-deck dry cargo steamers, the first of these being the BARON INVERCLYDE in 1954, followed by the BARON ARDROSSAN, BARON GLENCONNER, BARON INCHCAPE, BARON OGILVY and BARON BERWICK, all of which were in service by 1956. This building programme was closely followed by another when, in 1958, the first of eight 10,500-ton deadweight, diesel-engined 'tween-deck dry cargo ships, the BARON JEDBURGH, went into service. Between that year and 1960 the remainder, BARON GARIOCH, BARON KINNAIRD, BARON MACLAY, BARON MINTO, BARON PENTLAND, BARON WEMYSS and BARON BELHAVEN, entered service.

The years between 1957 (December) and 1963 (February) found the Company engaged — in common with many other tramping companies — in the carriage of a type of cargo not normally associated with tramp vessels, namely motor cars. It was during this period, when the small and medium-sized British car became quite popular for the first time in the United States and Canada, that all available shipping space was required to lift the cars earmarked for export and this resulted in many thousands of cars being transported to the East, Gulf and West Coasts of North America. However, even before that, in the period following shortly after the Second World War — April, 1949 to be precise — one of the Company's ships, the BARON HAIG, created history by bringing to the United Kingdom (London) the first bulk sugar cargo ever to be imported into this country, thus heralding the start of a revolution in the carriage to and handling of raw sugar in this country. It was the first of hundreds of individual bulk sugar cargoes brought

m.v. BARON WEMYSS (III)   Turners, Newcastle-on-Tyne

to the United Kingdom in 'Baron' ships and between April, 1951 (when this method of carrying sugar was in full flood) and mid-1967 (the period when the Company was prominently engaged in this trade) the total tonnage imported into the United Kingdom in Company ships exceeded, by a considerable margin, two million tons.

In 1963 James Pollock (born 1901), John Percy Walkinshaw (born 1920) and Walter Marshall Scott (born 1920) joined the Board of H. Hogarth and Sons Limited and, also in 1963, Alastair Herbert Menzies Halliday (born 1917) and Donald Brant (born 1924) were appointed Directors of Hogarth Sons and Company Limited.

In January, 1965 four ships were owned by Kelvin Shipping Company Limited, the BARON BERWICK, BARON GARIOCH, BARON PENTLAND and BARON WEMYSS, and on the 5th of that month the latter three were sold to Hogarth Shipping Company Limited and later in the same month the BARON BERWICK, the last but one of the post-war built steamers remaining in the fleet, was disposed of to foreign buyers. Then, on 3rd February, 1965 Kelvin Shipping Company Limited was placed in Members' Voluntary Liquidation and on 1st January, 1966 H. Hogarth and Sons Limited and Hogarth Sons and Company Limited became wholly-owned subsidiaries of Hogarth Shipping Company Limited and at the same time the ships were transferred from Hogarth Shipping Company Limited to H. Hogarth and Sons Limited.

On 1st April, 1966 Maxwell Bellingham Cheales (born 1929), the son-in-law of Hugh Hogarth, Chairman and Managing Director at the time, joined the Board of Hogarth Shipping Company Limited and on 31st December of that year James Pollock retired from the Board of H. Hogarth and Sons Limited.

9

It was in December, 1965 that the Company's first dry cargo bulk carrier, m.v. BARON INVERFORTH, joined the fleet and heralded the beginning of a change in the type of ship operated by the Company. With increasing rapidity during the post-war years the pattern of world trading was changing meaning, in the case of tramp shipping, that the bulk carrier with engines aft was becoming more and more acceptable as a class to charterers whilst the role of 'tween-decker with engines amidships was declining. This had the unfortunate effect of reducing the attraction in world markets of the Company's diesel-engined 'tweendeckers and it was therefore decided to dispose of them, at the same time instituting a bulk carrier building programme.

This decision resulted in orders being placed with Norwegian builders for the undernoted ships:

1967	BARON FORBES	19,861 tons deadweight	at Haugesund
1968	BARON CAWDOR	21,950 tons deadweight	at Horten
1968	BARON DUNMORE	19,958 tons deadweight	at Haugesund
1970	BARON RENFREW	22,200 tons deadweight	at Horten
1970	BARON ARDROSSAN	23,655 tons deadweight	at Haugesund
1971	BARON INCHCAPE	23,700 tons deadweight	at Haugesund
1971	BARON BELHAVEN	23,340 tons deadweight	at Tønsberg
1971	BARON MACLAY	21,950 tons deadweight	at Horten
1972	BARON WEMYSS	23,710 tons deadweight	at Haugesund

Reference to the individual Ship Histories will provide details of these ships.

On 12th February, 1968 a change of very considerable importance took place when the Directors of H. Hogarth and Sons Limited and Lyle Shipping Company Limited, Glasgow, announced the formation of a Joint Management Company to be called Scottish Ship Management Limited. The share capital of this Company has, since its formation, been held in equal proportions by the two Parent Companies.

The Directors appointed to Scottish Ship Management Limited at the time of the Company's formation were Mr John P. Walkinshaw and Mr Walter M. Scott, from Hogarth, and Mr Thomas S. Shearer and Mr Herbert A. Walkinshaw, from Lyle. The Staff, both shore and seagoing, was drawn from the staffs of the Parent Companies. From 1927 the offices of H. Hogarth and Sons Limited were situated at 120 St. Vincent Street, Glasgow, but on the formation of Scottish Ship Management Limited that Company, Lyle and Hogarth opened adjacent offices at 40 and 48 Buchanan Street, Glasgow.

In view of this reorganisation and the need for less restricted representation which resulted, the London Offices of Hogarth and Sons and Company Limited were closed in April, 1968, although that Company continues in existence. At that time Alastair H. Halliday and Donald Brant relinquished their Directorships with Hogarth Sons and Company Limited.

The ships of the Hogarth and Lyle fleets continue to be owned by the respective Parent Companies and to sail under their names of 'Barons' and 'Capes' but the Management Company does have its own House Flag which all the vessels of the two fleets fly. Originally, this flag was blue (the shade of blue being that of the Lyle House Flag) with a red band (the shade of red being that of the Hogarth House Flag) top and bottom. On the blue field, in the centre of the flag, a white roundel appeared within which was an interwoven red 'H' and blue 'L'. In 1974, after the holding of a competition amongst the seagoing and shore staff for a new design of House Flag, a new flag was adopted. The main field of this flag is dark blue and upon this is a white triangle, or 'pennant' portion. Within the triangle, in red, are the letters 'SSM'. In addition to flying this flag, all the ships continue to fly the St. Andrew's Cross as they have done for many years, thereby emphasising their Scottish connections. The Hogarth House Flag is still to be seen on 'Baron' ships, however, in the form of a plaque carried on the bows.

The colour scheme of the ships remains unaltered, being grey topsides with red boot-topping, white superstructure and boats and buff masts, deck-houses, cranes, etc. The funnel is buff with a black top and on each side of the funnel is a blue seahorse, this small marine creature being the emblem of Scottish Ship Management Limited. The hull colour was changed from black to grey in 1960, the first ship of the fleet to appear in grey being BARON JEDBURGH (III).

On 1st September, 1970 H. Hogarth and Sons Limited placed an order with Upper Clyde Shipbuilders Limited, Glasgow for two 27,500 tons deadweight bulk carriers which, at the time of ordering, were expected to enter service between 1972 and 1973. However, with Upper Clyde Shipbuilders Limited going into liquidation in 1971, these ships never materialised and this was an unhappy incident which, fortunately, remains unique in the history of the Company.

On 1st January, 1971 Herbert Laird Brodie (born 1920), Manager of the Agency Department of H. Hogarth and Sons Limited, was appointed a Director of that Company and on 1st July of that year Maxwell Bellingham Cheales, a Director of Hogarth Shipping Company Limited, was appointed Managing Director of that Company and subsequently of H. Hogarth and Sons Limited. Also, on that date, Dr Hugh Crawford Hogarth (born 1948), the only son of Hugh Hogarth who, at that time, was Chairman of the Hogarth Group of Companies, was appointed a Director of Hogarth Shipping Company Limited. Dr Hogarth practices medicine in England.

The following year, on 27th April, 1972, Donald Charles Macpherson (born 1932), a Partner with Fielding, Newson-Smith and Company, Stockbrokers in London, was appointed a Director of Hogarth Shipping Company Limited.

Hugh Hogarth 1909-1973

The Organisation suffered a severe blow when, on 12th August, 1973 the Chairman, Hugh Hogarth, died. He was born on 29th June, 1909, and after leaving Oxford University he joined H. Hogarth and Sons in 1930 and was assumed a Partner in 1935. After the Second World War Mr Hogarth took a leading part in re-establishing the Company's fleet and his contribution to Shipping generally, both at a national and local level, was very real. The amount of work he did, over a long period of years, for the Chamber of Shipping of the United Kingdom was immense and he became a member of the Council of the Chamber of Shipping in 1948 and was Chairman of the Documentary Committee from 1948 until 1959 and again from 1961 until 1963. He was also Chairman of the Deep Sea Tramp Section in 1956-1957 and 1958-1959 and was elected President of the Chamber of Shipping of the United Kingdom in 1960. In 1954 he was President of the Glasgow Shipowners' and Shipbrokers' Benevolent Association and in 1959 was a Joint Vice-Chairman of the former General Council of British Shipping. From 1966 until 1969 he was Chairman of the Shipowners' Panel, Northern Lights Conference. He was a Director of The North of England Protecting and Indemnity Association Limited from 1949 until his death in 1973 and Chairman of that organisation between 1968 and 1970.

Mr Alastair Crawford Hogarth was appointed Chairman of the Hogarth Group of Companies in succession to his late brother, and on 28th June, 1974 Mr John P. Walkinshaw, a Director of H. Hogarth and Sons Limited, Hogarth Sons and Company Limited and Scottish Ship Management Limited, joined the Board of Hogarth Shipping Company Limited.

In December, 1973 contracts were signed with Govan Shipbuilders Limited, Glasgow, for the building of two bulk carriers of approximately 26,000 tons deadweight each and these vessels have been christened BARON NAPIER and BARON PENTLAND. Delivery of both took place in June, 1976. Indeed, this was a unique occasion in the history of the Company — two ships, both built by the same Clyde shipbuilders, delivered on the same day (24th June) and within an hour of each other.

In addition, in August, 1975 an order was placed with Mitsui Shipbuilding and Engineering Company, Chiba, Japan, for one 32,000 tons deadweight bulk carrier which is to be delivered during April, 1977. She will be christened BARON MURRAY.

With this continuing policy of building new ships, it is apparent that the principal activity of the Hogarth Group of Companies remains shipowning, but the decision was taken some time ago to diversify into other fields of activity and by so doing remain abreast of events in an ever-changing world.

The first move in this direction came in May, 1972 when, with Lyle Shipping Company and others, Hogarth Shipping Company Limited formed Seaforth Maritime Limited in Aberdeen, an organisation engaged chiefly in supplying and servicing oil rigs, initially in the North Sea, but subsequently operating over a much wider area of the world. This is a very progressive company which, having commenced with four supply vessels, now has in operation or building a total of twelve vessels. In addition, Seaforth has taken over or formed other companies which enables it to offer a very comprehensive service to the Oil Industry. In particular, the Company has a major interest in Barry, Henry and Cook Limited, one of Aberdeen's oldest engineering companies, which is becoming increasingly involved in the manufacture of diving systems for use in the North Sea. Mr M. B. Cheales is one of the Directors of Seaforth Maritime Limited.

On 1st April, 1972 Hogarth Shipping Company Limited acquired jointly, with Lyle Shipping Company Limited, the whole of the share capital of John Kilgour and Company Limited, an old-established shipbroking firm in London, and this Company was made a subsidiary of Scottish Ship Management Limited later that year. Kilgour is responsible for a major part of the chartering of both the Hogarth and Lyle fleets.

In 1973 a subsidiary company of Hogarth Shipping Company Limited came into being — Hogarth Shipping Estates Limited — whose function is to acquire good commercial property in various areas where it is anticipated that there is likely to be a continuing demand for office accommodation. The Directors of this Company are Mr A. C. Hogarth, Mr M. B. Cheales, Mr D. C. Macpherson and Mr John Neil Maclean. Mr Maclean (born 1944) joined the Hogarth Group of Companies in September, 1972. On 29th April, 1976 he was appointed a Director of Hogarth Shipping Company Limited and H. Hogarth and Sons Limited.

The year 1973 (February) also saw the acquisition by Hogarth Shipping Company Limited of an old-established Glasgow firm of travel and ships' agents, T. L. Duff and Company Limited, with premises well placed in the centre of the business area of Glasgow. For administrative reasons the business was divided into two separate organisations — T. L. Duff and Company Limited and T. L. Duff and Company (Ships' Agency) Limited. Certain of the Hogarth Directors are Directors of T. L. Duff and Company Limited and T. L. Duff and Company (Ship's Agency) Limited, namely M. B. Cheales, H. L. Brodie, D. C. Macpherson and J. N. Maclean. In August, 1974 T. L. Duff and Company Limited expanded its area of operations beyond Glasgow by opening a branch office in Montrose, Angus, a town which is benefitting considerably from the North Sea oil business. Further expansion came about in December, 1974 when the Inverness travel firm of Ness Travel was acquired.

T. L. Duff and Company Limited was originally established in Hope Street, Glasgow, on 1st August, 1896 by Thomas Lawrie Duff as Insurance Brokers and Commission Agents. The following year they also became shipowners with the building of the s.s. MAYFLOWER and the formation of the Mayflower Steamship Company Limited. The Company ceased to own ships some years prior to the outbreak of war in 1939.

In conclusion, it must be placed on record that the Hogarth family has guided the Company continuously for one hundred years and progress over these years has meant that the Hogarth name remains in the forefront of World Shipping today. The momentum to ensure this progress has been generated and sustained by the foresight, sound judgement and unstinting effort of the Directors and Staff of whom many, past and present, have spent most — and in some cases all — their working lives with the Company.

FLEET LIST

FLEET LIST NOTES

The notation 'I', 'II', etc, in brackets after a ship's name indicates that she is the first, second, etc, ship of that name in the fleet. The dates following the name are those of entering and leaving the fleet. Ships are steel-hulled unless otherwise stated. The Official Number is the number given by the British Registrar of Shipping, and remains unchanged during the life of a ship under the British flag. WESTERN CHIEF was one of the very few not to have one, being lost before a number could be allocated to her. Tonnages are gross — 'g', net — 'n', and, for ships in the present fleet, deadweight — 'd'. The dimensions given are the registered length x beam x depth in feet and tenths of a foot up to ship number 128, thereafter they are the overall length x beam x draught at summer deadweight. The ships' histories are corrected up to July 1976.

1. KATE. In the fleet from 1870 to 1877.
Official No. 3386. 171 tons gross, 154 tons net. Length 91.5 x 23.0 beam x 12.8 feet depth. Wood Brig.
1852: Built at Bathurst N.B. *1867:* Owned by J. Brown, Bathurst N.B. *1870:* Purchased by John Hogarth, elder brother of Hugh Hogarth and managed by Goodwin & Hogarth. *1877:* Sold to S. Savage, Ayr. *1886:* Broken up.

2. JESSIE GOODWIN (1873-1875)
ON.64016. 357g, 338n. 129.6 x 29.4 x 12.9 feet. Wood Barque.
1871: Completed by R.Hawkinson, Weymouth N.S. for their own account. *26.4.1873:* Purchased by Goodwin & Hogarth. *1875:* Wholly owned by James Goodwin. *19.1.1887:* Wrecked in Downings Bay, Co.Donegal, whilst on passage from Troon to Limerick.

3. EMMA L. OULTON (1873-1876)
ON.64553. 660n. 146.2 x 32.4 x 18.3 feet. Wood Barque.
8.1871: Completed by H. Purdy, Sackville N.B. for Oulton Bros. of that port. *6.1873:* Purchased by H. Hogarth. *12.3.1876:* Abandoned in the North Atlantic, in position 37N. 60W., whilst on passage from Baltimore to Cork with corn, improperly stowed. Six of her crew of 20 were lost.

4. BRISK (1874-1877)
ON.55841. 296g, 284n. 120.0 x 27.8 x 12.7 feet. Wood Brigantine.
1868: Completed by Muir, Shelburne, N.S., for W. Muir, Shelburne. *1874:* Purchased by Goodwin & Hogarth. *14.11.1877:* Abandoned in the North Atlantic.

5. BURNBRAE (1874-1875)
ON.54437. 339g, 320n. 127.8 x 29.8 x 12.9 feet. Wood Barque.
11.1866: Completed by W. & R. Wallace, Gardiners Creek, N.B. for W. McLean & Co., St. John, N.B. *1874:* Purchased by Goodwin & Hogarth. *3.1875:* Hogarth interest sold. *11.1.1878:* Foundered in position 10.46N., 58.53W., whilst on passage from Georgetown, British Guiana to Queenstown with timber.

6. JANE YOUNG (1874-1876)
ON.46923. 463g, 439n. 131.0 x 30.7 x 17.3 feet. Wood Barque.
1863: Completed by Abraham Young, Granville N.S. for J. V. Troop, St. John N.B. *24.1.1874:* Purchased by Goodwin & Hogarth. *2.7.1874:* Dismasted in heavy seas — crew rescued by Southport lifeboat. *12.5.1876:* Stranded on South coast of Langlois Island, Miquelon, whilst on passage from Ardrosan to Quebec.

7. G. A. COONAN (1874-1881)
ON.52116. 299g, 279n. 116.7 x 29.0 x 12.0 feet. Wood Brigantine.
1865: Completed by S. V. Coonan, Harvey N.B. for Coonan & Co., St. John N.B. *1867:* Sold to William Menely, St. John N.B. *3.2.1874:* Purchased by Goodwin & Hogarth. *4.5.1881:* Sold to Fritz Iversen, Denmark and renamed BELLONA. *10.10.1892:* Foundered in the North Sea.

8. JOSEPHINE (1874-1878)
ON.46947. 474g, 457n. 133.0 x 29.9 x 17.0 feet. Wood Barque.
1863: Completed by Flewelling, St. John N.B. for J. V. Troop of that port. *1874:* Purchased by Goodwin & Hogarth. *1878:* Sold to J. Curwen, Maryport. *17.5.1882:* Abandoned waterlogged in position 53N. 32W., after springing a leak, whilst on passage from Workington to Quebec with coal.

9. MYSTIC TIE (1876-1877)
ON.69198. 345g, 313n. 115.0 x 30.0 x 12.8 feet. Wood Brigantine.
2.9.1874: Completed by R. P. Trefery, La Have N.S. for Goodwin & Hogarth. *11.11.1877:* Wrecked near St. David's.

10. MARY HOGARTH (1875-1889)

ON.72232. 623g, 588n. 143.6 x 32.2 x 18.0 feet. Wood Barque.
1875: Completed by W. & R. Wallace, Gardiner's Creek, N.B. for Goodwin & Hogarth. *21.6.1889:* Sold to C. M. Tollisen, Norway and renamed NORGE. *26.9.1889:* Abandoned in position 5N. 20W., after her cargo of coal had caught fire during a voyage from Grangemouth to Montevideo.

11. DRUMADOON (1877-1886)

ON.73469. 926g, 866n. 172.3 x33.9 x20.3 feet. Wood Barque.
10.10.1876: Completed by Lawrence Delap & Co., Annapolis N.S. for their own account. *1877:* Purchased by Goodwin & Hogarth. *1878:* Allocated to Hugh Hogarth on dissolution of partnership. *26.11.1886:* Destroyed by fire at Galveston, whilst loading cotton for Liverpool.

12. CYPRUS (1878-1881)

ON.79626. 533g, 500n. 150.5 x 29.6 x 17.2 feet. Wood Barque.
1878: Completed by Jas. D. Warlow, Llanstadwell, Neyland, for Hugh Hogarth. *1881:* Sold to Alex. Blaney, Belfast. Later registered under John Monaghan, Master of the vessel, who was given power to sell the ship within twelve months for £4,000. *13.3.1883:* Left Newcastle N.S.W. for Bangkok and disappeared.

13. MODERN (1878-1882)

ON.75659. 770g, 741n. 161.0 x 32.5 x 20.0 feet. Wood Barque.
1877: Completed by P. Baldwin, Quebec for his own account. *1878:* Purchased by Hugh Hogarth. *30.6.1882:* Destroyed by fire in position 32S. 64E., whilst on passage from South Shields to Anjer with coal. All crew of fifteen and two passengers were lost.

14. BRUSSELS (1882-1891)

ON.45969. 991g, 991n. 211.3 x 31.9 x 21.5 feet. Iron Barque.
5.1863: Completed by Charles Connell, Glasgow as CITY OF BRUSSELS for George Smith & Sons, Glasgow. *1882:* Purchased by Hugh Hogarth and renamed BRUSSELS. *1891:* Sold to Shaw, Savill & Co., London, name unchanged. *1903:* Sold to Niger Co. Ltd., London and by *7.1904* hulked in West Africa.

s.s. BARON ARDROSSAN (I)   *From a painting*

15. BARON ARDROSSAN (I) (1881-1891)

ON.79425. 1,451g, 917n. 243.5 x 34.0 x 17.9 feet. Iron Steamship.
Compound 2-cylinder steam engines of 168 nominal horse power, by Blair & Co. Ltd., Stockton.
4.1881: Completed by Thomas Turnbull & Son, Whitby. *1891:* Sold to J. C. Bonnin, France and renamed EMILE. *1895:* Sold to T. Weissenburger (L. Doménil-Leblé manager), France. *1898:* Sold to P. Rowe and Sons, Cardiff and renamed BARON ARDROSSAN. *21.8.1898:* Wrecked near Fishguard, whilst on passage from Glasgow to St. Malo.

16. BARON CLYDE (1883-1893)

ON.86062. 1,806g, 1,155n. 260.4 x 37.1 x 18.5 feet. Iron Steamship.
C. 2-cyl. (160 nhp.) by Blair & Co. Ltd., Stockton.
6.1883: Completed by Thomas Turnbull & Son, Whitby. *1893:* Sold to F. Rahtkens & Co., Germany. *1895:* Sold to Aktieselskabet "Baron Clyde" (F. Ohlsen manager), Norway. *1898:* Sold to Solleveld, van der Meer and van Hattum, Holland and renamed MOERDYK. *10.7.1904:* Whilst on passage from Huelva to Rotterdam with iron pyrites, she was in collision with the s.s. PHOSPHOR in the Bay of Biscay, and both vessels were lost.

17. IBERIA (1883-1889)
ON.60622. 1,072g, 675n. 230.0 x 30.1 x 21.6 feet. Iron Steamship.
C. 2-cyl. (115 nhp.) by the Shipbuilders.
4.1871: Completed by Blackwood & Gordon, Port Glasgow for Anderson & Son, Ardrossan. *1873:* Sold to Henderson & Sons, Ardrossan. *1876:* Sold to Ardrossan S.S. Co. *1883:* Purchased by Hugh Hogarth. *1889:* Sold to Napier Shipping Co. *1896:* Sold to J. Ribère & Cie., France and renamed ALGERIEN. *1899:* Sold to Devoto & Beraldo, Italy and renamed RICORDO. *1901:* Sold to S. A. Siderides, Russia and renamed SULTANA. *1903:* Transferred to Greek flag. *14.1.1905:* Foundered 20 miles off Adalia, whilst on passage from Payas to Copenhagen via Messina with oranges.

18. MACHRIHANISH (1883-1908)
ON.86064. 1,758g, 1,699n. 264.9 x 39.8 x 23.4 feet. Iron 3-masted Ship.
9.1883: Completed by Robert Duncan, Port Glasgow. *1908:* Sold to Acties. Avance (S. Marcussen manager), Norway and renamed AVANCE. *2.6.1911:* Wrecked on Lobos Island, whilst on passage from Lobos de Tierra to the U.K. or the Continent with guano.

s.v. OCHTERTYRE   *From a painting by Montague Dawson*

19. OCHTERTYRE (1885-1910)
ON.86069. 1,354g, 1,263n. 239.5 x 36.2 x 21.5 feet. Iron Barque.
7.1885: Completed by Robert Duncan & Co., Port Glasgow. *1910:* Sold to Akties. Kosmos (C. Christensen manager), Norway and renamed HAVFRUEN. *3.12.1911:* Sunk by ice in position 58.21S., 31.07W., whilst on passage from South Georgia (in tow) to the Sandwich Group.

20. CORRYVRECHAN (1885-1909)
ON.92871. 1,356g, 1,266n. 240.0 x 36.2 x 21.5 feet. Steel Barque.
9.1885: Completed by Robert Duncan & Co., Port Glasgow. *1909:* Sold to T. Dannevig & Co., Norway and renamed SVENOR. *21.5.1914:* Abandoned off Tasmania, whilst on passage from South Georgia to Newcastle N.S.W. in ballast.

21. BARON BELHAVEN (I) (1887-1900)
ON.92877. 2,356g, 1,511n. 300.5 x 40.0 x 21.9 feet. Steel Steamship.
Triple expansion 3-cyl. steam engines (200 nhp) by Duncan Stewart & Co., Glasgow.
8.1887: Completed by Robert Duncan & Co., Port Glasgow. *1898:* Registered under the Hogarth Shipping Co. Ltd. *1900:* Sold to H. Svanoe, Norway and renamed GLITRA. *10.8.1916:* Wrecked at Huxter, Sandnaes, Shetland Islands, whilst on passage from Baltimore to Skien with rye, barley and wheat.

22. WESTFALIA.(1887-1889)
ON.86690. 1,135g, 720n. 241.0 x 33.4 x 13.9 feet. Iron Steamship.
C. 2-cyl. (130 nhp) by Fleming & Ferguson, Paisley.
7.1882: Completed by William Hamilton & Co., Port Glasgow for Walker, Donald & Co., Glasgow. *1887:* Sold to R. H. Elder and management of the vessel taken over by Hugh Hogarth. *4.2.1889:* Wrecked near Corunna, whilst on passage from Huelva to Garston.

23. BARON DOUGLAS (I) (1888-1899)
ON.92879. 2,700g, 1,725n. 302.3 x 40.2 x 23.5 feet. Steamship.
T. 3-cyl. (211 nhp) by the Shipbuilders.
10.1888: Completed by Blackwood & Gordon, Port Glasgow. *1898:* Registered under Hogarth Shipping Co. Ltd. *1899:* Sold to Cia. Cantabrica de Nav., Spain and renamed OROZCO. *25.2.1915:* Foundered about 50 miles off La Rochelle, whilst on passage from Bilbao to Middlesbrough with iron ore..

24. BARON ELIBANK (I) (1889-1899)
ON.92880. 1,772g, 1,147n. 259.7 x 37.0 x 15.0 feet. Steamship.
T. 3-cyl. (171 nhp) by Duncan Stewart & Co., Glasgow.
1889: Completed by Murdoch & Murray, Port Glasgow. *1898:* Registered under the Hogarth Shipping Co. Ltd. *1899:* Sold to Delmas Frères, France and renamed FORT-LOUIS. *28.5.1910:* Lost in collision with s.s. HILDAWELL 6 miles west of the Longships, whilst on passage from Cardiff to Tunis with patent fuel.

25. BARON FIFE (1890-1894)
ON.97561. 1,310g, 816n. 230.0 x 33.1 x 13.7 feet. Steamship.
T. 3-cyl. (134 nhp) by Duncan Stewart & Co., Glasgow.
2.1890: Completed by R. Duncan & Co., Port Glasgow. *1894:* Sold to L. Balande fils ainé, France and renamed ST. LOUIS. *1900:* Sold to Union Commerciale et de Nav. Calédonienne, Noumea, France. *1926:* Sold to Cie. "Le Nickel", Noumea. *1930:* Sold to Soc. du Tour de Côtes, Noumea, and used as a barge for carrying ore to Noumea. *1933:* Hulked off Ducos promontory, Noumea and left to rot.

26. ARDNAMURCHAN (1890-1909)
ON.97562. 1,718g, 1,619n. 259.4 x 38.1 x 23.1 feet. 3-masted Ship.
22.5.1890: Launched. *6.1890:* Completed by Russell & Co., Port Glasgow. *1909:* Sold to P. Schiaffino fu P., Italy and renamed SPERANZA. *1912:* Sold to Akties. Gunda (Th. Brovig manager), Norway and renamed GUNDA. *1926:* Broken up in Holland.

27. BARON ARDROSSAN (II) (1892-1904)
ON.97563. 2,823g, 1,825n. 309.2 x 40.6 x 17.6 feet. Steamship.
T. 3-cyl (249 nhp) by T. Richardson & Sons, Hartlepool.
1.1892: Completed by Raylton Dixon & Co., Middlesbrough. *1898:* Registered under Hogarth Shipping Co. Ltd. *1904:* Sold to Diederichsen, Jebsen & Co., Germany and renamed POSCHAN. *1907:* Sold to K. Fujioka, Japan and renamed KOKO MARU. *23.10.1907:* Wrecked at Ainoshima, whilst on passage from Saigon to Yokohama with rice.

s.v. BALLACHULISH as 'Sandvigen'

28. BALLACHULISH (1892-1909)
ON.97565. 1,901g, 1,751n. 265.2 x 40.0 x 23.0 feet. 3-masted Ship.
8.1892: Completed by A. Rodger & Co., Port Glasgow. *1909:* Sold to Sven O. Stray & Co., Norway and renamed SANDVIGEN. *12.1923:* Sold to the S.A. des Hauts Fourneaux de Noumea, France. *1924:* Hulked in New Caledonia.

29. COLINTRAIVE (1892-1894)
ON.97566. 1,907g, 1,747n. 265.3 x 40.0 x 23.0 feet. 3-masted Ship.
10.1892: Completed by A. Rodger & Co., Port Glasgow. *16.3.1894:* Left Newcastle N.S.W. for San Francisco with a cargo of coal and disappeared.

30. BARON GLAMIS (1894-1903)
ON.97568. 2,432g, 1,556n. 301.2 x 40.6 x 16.7 feet. Steamship.
T. 3-cyl. (206 nhp) by J. G. Kincaid & Co. Ltd., Greenock.
7.1894: Completed by A. Rodger & Co., Port Glasgow. *1898:* Registered under Hogarth Shipping Co. Ltd. *21.1.1903:* Wrecked 3 miles South of Corsewall Lighthouse, Wigtownshire, whilst on passage from Glasgow to Buenos Ayres with coals.

31. BARON HUNTLY (1894-1906)
ON.97569. 1,398g, 866n. 235.9 x 33.4 x 15.0 feet.
T. 3-cyl. (144 nhp) by J. G. Kincaid & Co. Ltd., Greenock.
12.1894: Completed by A. Rodger & Co., Port Glasgow. *1898:* Transferred to Hogarth Shipping Co. Ltd. *1904:* Transferred to Kelvin Shipping Co. Ltd. *28.10.1906:* Abandoned 10 miles S.W. of Cabo Raso, Portugal, whilst on passage from Huelva to Dublin with copper ore.

s.s. BARON CAWDOR (I)   *W. Robertson & Co., Gourock*

32. BARON CAWDOR (I) (1895-1904)
ON.97570. 3,192g, 2,053n. 325.5 x 43.1 x 19.8 feet.
T. 3-cyl. (306 nhp) by Dunsmuir & Jackson, Glasgow.
1.1895: Completed by A. Rodger & Co., Port Glasgow. *1898:* Transferred to Hogarth Shipping Co. Ltd. *1904:* Sold to Kishimoto Kanetaro, Japan and renamed SHINSHU MARU. *10.9.1911:* Foundered off Hainan Island, whilst on passage from Miike to Singapore with coal.

33. BARON INNERDALE (1896-1914)
ON.105252. 3,344g, 2,140n. 335.0 x 43.5 x 27.2 feet.
T. 3-cyl. (292 nhp) by Dunsmuir & Jackson, Glasgow.
1896: Completed by A. Rodger & Co., Port Glasgow. *1898:* Transferred to the Hogarth Shipping Co. Ltd. *27.10.1914:* Lost in collision in the Red Sea with s.s. AFRICAN MONARCH, whilst on passage from Port Said to Calcutta with salt.

s.s. BARON INNERDALE at Perim 1904

34. BARON FAIRLIE (I) (1898-1920)
ON.105255. 3,599g, 2,324n. 354.6 x 45.0 x 25.9 feet.
T. 3-cyl. (310 nhp) by Dunsmuir & Jackson, Glasgow.
1898: Completed by A. Rodger & Co., Port Glasgow for the Hogarth Shipping Co. Ltd. *1920:* Sold to the Esperia S.S. Co. Ltd. (Ockenden & Son managers), London and renamed ESPERIA. *1924:* Sold to Orders & Handford S.S. Co. Ltd. (J. Cory & Sons Ltd. managers), Cardiff. *1927:* Sold to V. Saglimbene, Italy and renamed CISCATO. *1933:* Sold to G. Riccardi, Italy for breaking up.

s.s. BARON ELDON   *M. Barnard, Hull*

35. BARON ELDON (1899-1911)
ON.105256. 3,705g, 2,385n. 340.0 x 48.0 x 17.9 feet.
T. 3-cyl. (314 nhp) by J. Dickinson & Sons Ltd., Sunderland.
9.1899: Completed by Bartram & Sons, Sunderland for the Hogarth Shipping Co. Ltd. *1911:* Sold to Meiji Kaiun Kabushiki Kaisha, Japan and renamed TOKAI MARU. *1915:* Sold to Okazaki Kisen Kabushiki Kaisha, Japan. *1917:* Sold to Kabushiki Kaisha Nansho Yoko, Japan. *1920:* Sold to A. Bistis & Co. Ltd., Greece and renamed THEOFANO. *1921:* Sold to Byron S.S. Co. Ltd. (M. A. Embiricos manager), London and renamed MAID OF MILOS. *1924:* Sold to H. W. Retschen, Germany for breaking up. *4.4.1924:* Arrived at Wilhelmshaven for demolition.

36. BARON DALMENY (I) (1900-1919)
ON.105257. 3,899g, 2,522n. 354.4 x 48.1 x 25.8 feet.
T. 3-cyl. (310 nhp) by Dunsmuir & Jackson, Glasgow.
1900: Completed by A. Rodger & Co., Port Glasgow for the Hogarth Shipping Co. Ltd. *1919:* Sold to Kjeld Stubs Dampskibs Selskab, Norway and renamed NANNA STUB. *1922:* Sold to Forenede Rederier A/S (Gorrissen & Co. A/S managers), Norway and renamed ELVENES. *1925:* Sold to D/S A/S Brommelands Rederi (S. Brommeland manager), Norway and renamed ELVEN. *26.10.1925:* Abandoned in the North Atlantic, whilst on passage from Rotterdam to Sydney C.B. with general cargo.

37. BARON BALFOUR (1901-1917)
ON.105258. 3,991g, 2,552n. 358.8 x 48.1 x 25.6 feet.
T. 3-cyl. (320 nhp) by Dunsmuir & Jackson, Glasgow.
1901: Completed by A. Rodger & Co., Port Glasgow for the Hogarth Shipping Co. Ltd. *28.10.1917:* Torpedoed and sunk by U-46 8 miles North from Sein Island, Murmanski Coast.

38. BARON KELVIN (I) (1903-1913)
ON.105260. 1,591g, 891n. 245.0 x 35.6 x 20.6 feet.
T. 3-cyl. (162 nhp) by Dunsmuir & Jackson, Glasgow.
1903: Completed by Charles Connell & Co. Ltd., Glasgow for the Kelvin Shipping Co. Ltd. *1913:* Sold to the Atlantic & Eastern S.S. Co. Ltd. (J. Glynn & Son managers), Liverpool and renamed COSTELLO. *3.8.1915:* Sunk 95 miles West by South of Bishop Rock by gunfire from U.28.

s.s. **BARON DALMENY (I)** *World Ship Photo Library*

39. BARON GORDON (1903-1904)
ON.118232. 4,236g, 2,703n. 375.0 x 49.5 x 26.5 feet.
T. 3-cyl. (320 nhp) by Dunsmuir & Jackson Ltd., Glasgow.
1903: Completed by Charles Connell & Co. Ltd., Glasgow for the Hogarth Shipping Co. Ltd.
31.7.1904: Wrecked on Bombay Reef, Paracel Islands, whilst on passage from Hong Kong to
Sourabaya in ballast.

40. BARON ARDROSSAN (III) (1905-1930)
ON.118233. 4,319g, 2,770n. 380.0 x 49.5 x 26.2 feet.
T. 3-cyl. (320 nhp) by Dunsmuir & Jackson Ltd., Glasgow.
1905: Completed by A. Rodger & Co., Port Glasgow for the Hogarth Shipping Co. Ltd. *5.8.1914-
18.8.1916:* Comissioned under the White Ensign as a Squadron Supply Ship Y9.8 and later
served as the collier Y3.1655. *3.1930:* Sold to J. M. Nickiforos and E. Z. Lemos, Greece and renamed
ARIADNE. *5.1934:* Sold to Italian shipbreakers. *23.6.1934:* Arrived at Spezia for demolition.

s.s. **BARON ARDROSSAN (III)** *C. Downs, Manchester*

41. BARON CAWDOR (II) (1905-1917)
ON.118234. 4,316g, 2,764n. 379.9 x 49.5 x 26.2 feet.
T. 3-cyl. (320 nhp) by Dunsmuir & Jackson Ltd., Glasgow.
1905: Completed by A. Rodger & Co., Port Glasgow for the Hogarth Shipping Co. Ltd. *9.6.1917:*
Torpedoed and sunk by U.96 150 miles S.W. by S. ½ S. from the Fastnet. Three of her crew were lost.

42. BARON LOVAT (I) (1906-1913)
ON.101980. 1,752g, 1,078n. 260.0 x 37.1 x 16.7 feet.
T. 3-cyl. (220 nhp) by G. Clark Ltd., Sunderland.
3.1893: Completed by J. Blumer & Co., Sunderland as SIBUN for Sibun S.S. Co. Ltd. (Scrutton, Sons & Co. managers), London. *1906:* Purchased by the Kelvin Shipping Co. Ltd. and renamed BARON LOVAT. *1913:* Sold to J. McL. Bell, Newcastle and renamed SHINON. *1914:* Sold to Shinon S.S. Co. Ltd. (Moller & Co. managers), Shanghai. *1922:* Sold to San Peh S.N. Co. Ltd., China. *1936:* Broken up.

s.s. **BARON HERRIES (I) on Trial Trip**

43. BARON HERRIES (I) (1907-1918)
ON.118238. 1,610g, 908n. 252.0 x 37.6 x 19.8 feet.
T. 3-cyl. (156 nhp) by D. Rowan & Co., Glasgow.
1907: Completed by Napier & Miller Ltd., Glasgow for the Kelvin Shipping Co. Ltd. *22.4.1918:* Torpedoed and sunk by U.91 43 miles N. by W. ½ W. from Bishop Rock. Three of her crew were lost.

44. BARON MINTO (I) (1908-1929)
ON.118239. 4,537g, 2,897n. 385.2 x 51.2 x 26.4 feet.
T. 3-cyl. (320 nhp) by Dunsmuir & Jackson Ltd., Glasgow.
1908: Completed by Napier & Miller Ltd., Glasgow for the Hogarth Shipping Co. Ltd. *8.1929:* Sold to Pithis Bros. & Co., Greece and renamed ADAMANTIOS J. PITHIS. *27.1.1940:* Wrecked off St. Ann's Head, near Milford Haven.

45. BARON GARIOCH (I) (1908-1917)
ON.102735. 1,831g, 1,129n. 265.0 x 37.6 x 17.5 feet.
T. 3-cyl. (156 nhp) by Central Marine Engine Works, West Hartlepool.
8.1895: Launched by William Gray & Co. Ltd., West Hartlepool as LADY OLIVIA for Shipping Agency Ltd. and then while completing purchased by J. R. Cuthbertson: thereafter being completed as KIRKSTALL for S.W. Furness, West Hartlepool. *1896:* Sold to J. E. Guthe, West Hartlepool. *1898:* Sold to West Hartlepool Steam Navigation Co. Ltd. *1908:* Purchased by the Kelvin Shipping Co. Ltd. and renamed BARON GARIOCH. *28.10.1917:* Torpedoed and sunk by submarine 5 miles S.E. from Anvil Point. Two of her crew were lost.

46. BARON OGILVY (I) (1909-1917)
ON.118240. 4,570g, 2,908n. 385.3 x 51.2 x 26.9 feet.
T. 3-cyl. (320 nhp) by D. Rowan & Co., Glasgow.
1909: Completed by A. Rodger & Co., Port Glasgow for the Hogarth Shipping Co. Ltd. *27.6.1917:* Torpedoed and sunk by submarine 172 miles N.W. from Tory Island. Two of her crew were lost.

47. BARON NAPIER (I) (1909-1926)
ON.128956. 4,943g, 3,159n. 400.3 x 52.3 x 27.4 feet.
T. 3-cyl. (369 nhp) by Dunsmuir & Jackson Ltd., Glasgow.
1909: Completed by Napier & Miller Ltd., Glasgow for the Hogarth Shipping Co. Ltd. *4.1926:* Sold to Oguma Koichiro, Japan and renamed ISHIN MARU. *1927:* Sold to Oguma Shoten Gomei Kaisha (Yoshida Jumushu manager), Japan. *1936:* Sold to Kyowa Kisen Kabushiki Kaisha, Japan. *1938:* Sold to Nissan Kisen K.K., Japan and renamed ISIN MARU. *1941:* Renamed NICHIWA MARU. *17.5.1944:* Sunk by the U.S. submarine TUNNY off the Ladrone Islands in position 14.45N., 142.40E.

48. BARON RENFREW (I) (1910-1932)
ON.128957. 1,605g, 874n. 275.0 x 40.1 x 17.0 feet.
T. 3-cyl. (156 nhp) by D. Rowan & Co., Glasgow.
1910: Completed by A. Rodger & Co., Port Glasgow for the Kelvin Shipping Co. Ltd. *1.1932:* Sold to Shaw Hsing S.S. Co. Ltd., China and renamed KUN HSING. *8.1937:* Sunk as a blockship in the Yangtse River.

49. BARON POLWARTH (I) (1911-1925)
ON.128958. 4,913g, 3,138n. 400.2 x 52.3 x 27.4 feet.
T. 3-cyl. (359 nhp) by Dunsmuir & Jackson Ltd., Glasgow.
1911: Completed by Napier & Miller Ltd., Glasgow for the Hogarth Shipping Co. Ltd. *1925:* Sold to Yamamoto Shoji K.K., Japan and renamed SHUNSEI MARU. *1938:* Name respelt SYUNSEI MARU. *1.4.1942:* Sunk by H.M.S. TRUANT in the Straits of Malacca west of Sumatra.

50. BARON SEMPILL (I) (1911-1917)
ON.128959. 1,607g, 868n. 275.3 x 40.1 x 17.0 feet.
T. 3-cyl. (156 nhp) by the Shipbuilders.
1911: Completed by A. Rodger & Co., Port Glasgow for the Kelvin Shipping Co. Ltd. *16.1.1917:* Captured by U.44 180 miles S.W. from the Fastnet and sunk by bombs.

51. BARON ERSKINE (I) (1911-1915)
ON.128960. 5,585g, 3,505n. 415.4 x 56.0 x 28.2 feet.
T. 3-cyl. (480 nhp) by D. Rowan & Co., Glasgow.
9.1911: Completed by A. MacMillan & Sons Ltd., Dumbarton for the Hogarth Shipping Co. Ltd., having been purchased whilst under construction as BEDLINGTON for the Bedlington S.S. Co. Ltd. (P.B. Pearson & Co. managers), Glasgow. *19.8.1915:* Torpedoed and sunk by U.38 25 miles N.N.W. from Bishop Rock.

s.s. BARON OGILVY (I)

s.s. BARON JEDBURGH (I)

52. BARON JEDBURGH (I) (1912-1930)
ON.128961. 4,418g, 2,684n. 410.0 x 54.3 x 24.8 feet.
T. 3-cyl. (400 nhp) by D. Rowan & Co., Glasgow.
1912: Completed by A. Rodger & Co., Port Glasgow for the Hogarth Shipping Co. Ltd. *1930:* Sold to T. J. Vatis, Greece and renamed IOANNIS VATIS. *3.1937:* Sold to Alpha S.S. Co. Ltd., London and renamed PECKHAM. *4.1939:* Sold to Johs. Fritzen & Sohn vorm W. Kunstmann, Germany and renamed JURGEN FRITZEN. *21.4.1940:* Sank near Landsort, about 50 miles South of Stockholm after grounding while on a voyage from Stettin to Stockholm.

53. BARON TWEEDMOUTH (I) (1912-1916)
ON.124030. 5,007g, 3,175n. 400.0 x 52.2 x 27.3 feet.
T. 3-cyl. (369 nhp) by Dunsmuir & Jackson Ltd., Glasgow.
1907: Completed by Napier & Miller Ltd., Glasgow as BELLE OF SCOTLAND for the Belle of Scotland S.S. Co. Ltd. (Crow, Rudolf & Co. managers), Liverpool. *1912:* Purchased by the Hogarth Shipping Co. Ltd. and renamed BARON TWEEDMOUTH. *30.5.1916:* Sunk by gunfire from U.34 25 miles N.E. by N. from Cape Carbon, Algeria.

54. BARON VERNON (I) (1912-1916)
ON.128962. 1,779g, 953n. 285.2 x 42.7 x 17.6 feet.
T. 3-cyl. (162 nhp) by Dunsmuir & Jackson Ltd., Glasgow.
1912: Completed by A. MacMillan & Sons Ltd., Dumbarton for the Kelvin Shipping Co. Ltd. *29.5.1916:* Sunk by gunfire from U.34 56 miles N.E. ½ N. from Algiers.

55. BARON AILSA (I) (1912-1918)
ON.128963. 1,836g, 1,153n. 279.2 x 40.1 x 18.8 feet.
T. 3-cyl. (175 nhp) by Richardsons, Westgarth & Co. Ltd., Middlesbrough.
1912: Completed by Greenock & Grangemouth Dockyard Co. Ltd., Grangemouth for the Kelvin Shipping Co. Ltd. having been purchased whilst under construction as EIBERGEN for N.V. Furness Scheepvaart en Agentuur Maatschappij (Furness, Withy & Co. Ltd. managers), Holland. *9.5.1918:* Torpedoed and sunk by submarine 18 miles W.N.W. from the Smalls, off Pembrokeshire. Ten of her crew were lost.

56. BARON WEMYSS (I) (1912-1917)
ON.128964. 1,605g, 865n. 275.3 x 40.1 x 17.0 feet.
T. 3-cyl. (156 nhp) by D. Rowan & Co., Glasgow.
1912: Completed by Dunlop, Bremner & Co. Ltd., Port Glasgow for the Kelvin Shipping Co. Ltd. *7.3.1917:* Torpedoed and sunk by submarine 73 miles N.W. x W. from the Fastnet. Two of her crew were lost.

57. BARON YARBOROUGH (I) (1913-1916)
ON.128965. 1,784g, 970n. 285.0 x 42.7 x 17.6 feet.
T. 3-cyl. (162 nhp) by Dunsmuir & Jackson Ltd., Glasgow.
1913: Completed by Napier & Miller Ltd., Glasgow for the Kelvin Shipping Co. Ltd. *1.9.1916:* Captured by U.34 27 miles N.W. from Dragonera Island, Majorca and sunk by bombs.

s.s. BARON BLANTYRE (I) on Government Service

58. BARON BLANTYRE (I) (1913-1917)
ON.127429. 1,844g, 1,138n. 276.5 x 40.6 x 18.6 feet.
T. 3-cyl. (175 nhp) by Dunsmuir & Jackson Ltd., Glasgow.
1908: Completed by Greenock & Grangemouth Dockyard Co. Ltd., Greenock as CASTLE EDEN for Furness, Withy & Co. Ltd., West Hartlepool. *1913:* Purchased by the Kelvin Shipping Co. Ltd. and renamed BARON BLANTYRE. *3.9.1917:* Torpedoed and sunk by submarine 60 miles N.W. ¾ W. from Cape Finisterre. One member of her crew was lost.

59. BARON KELVIN (II) (1915-1923)
ON.124349. 1,865g, 1,152n. 279.0 x 40.1 x 18.1 feet.
T. 3-cyl. (175 nhp) by MacColl & Pollock Ltd., Sunderland.
1907: Completed by Osbourne, Graham & Co., Sunderland as THIMBLEBY for Furness, Withy & Co. Ltd., West Hartlepool. *1915:* Purchased by the Kelvin Shipping Co. Ltd. and renamed BARON KELVIN. *1923:* Sold to British Invicta Shipping Co. Ltd. (Eggar, Forrester & Parker Ltd. managers), London and renamed L'INVICTA. *1923:* Sold to T. Murao, Japan and renamed TAKASAGO MARU. *1925:* Sold to Asahi Shokai K.K., Japan. *1931:* Sold to Sanbo Kisen Goshi Kaisha, Japan. *6.3.1932:* Wrecked in fog on the S.W. Coast of Korea, near Mokpo while on a voyage from Miike to Kunsan.

60. BARON CATHCART (1915-1924)
ON.124324. 1,860g, 1,162n. 279.3 x 40.1 x 18.1 feet.
T. 3-cyl. (190 nhp) by Richardsons, Westgarth & Co. Ltd., Sunderland.
1.1907: Completed by Osbourne, Graham & Co., Sunderland as WESTHAMPTON for the British Maritime Trust Ltd., West Hartlepool. *1907:* Sold to Furness, Withy & Co. Ltd., West Hartlepool. *1909:* Sold to Anglo-Hellenic S.S. Co. Ltd. (A. A. Embiricos & Co. managers), Greece and renamed ELLI. *1910:* Returned to Furness, Withy & Co. Ltd. and renamed WESTHAMPTON. *1913:* Sold to J. Gaff & Co., Glasgow and renamed AMPHION. *1915:* Purchased by the Kelvin Shipping Co. Ltd. and renamed BARON CATHCART. *1924:* Sold to the Seed Shipping Co. Ltd., Newcastle and renamed MARJORIE SEED. *25.12.1924:* Wrecked on the N.E. side of Lady Island, whilst on passage from Glasgow to Huelva with coal and coke.

61. BARON LOVAT (II) (1915-1917)
ON.135729. 5,604g, 3,582n. 423.5 x 56.0 x 28.7 feet.
T. 3-cyl. (555nhp.) by Rankin & Blackmore Ltd., Greenock.
5.1915: Completed by Russell & Co., Port Glasgow for the Hogarth Shipping Co. Ltd. *7.1917:* Sold to Prince Line Ltd. (Furness, Withy & Co. Ltd. managers), Newcastle and renamed SIBERIAN PRINCE. *12.1933:* Sold to L. A. Embiricos, Greece and renamed DUNAVIS. *1939:* Sold to I.N.S.A. (Industrie Navali Soc. Anon.), Italy and renamed ARLESIANA. *4.1943:* Abandoned at Tunis in a badly damaged condition. *29.5.1946:* Purchased by the Société Tunisienne de Sauvetage. *31.10.1946:* Refloated and subsequently sold to the British Iron & Steel Corporation Ltd. for breaking up. *21.10.1948:* Left Oran in tow for the River Tyne, where she was broken up by Clayton & Davie Ltd.

62. SAINT CECILIA. (1916).
ON.136265. 4,411g, 2,834n. 375.7 x 52.2 x 25.7 feet.
T. 3-cyl. (320nhp.) by Rankin & Blackmore Ltd., Glasgow.
1913: Completed by Greenock & Grangemouth Dockyard Co. Ltd., Greenock for the Saint Bride S.S. Co. Ltd. (A. Mackay & Co. managers), Glasgow. *1916:* Purchased by the Hogarth Shipping Co. Ltd., without change of name. *23.3.1916:* Sank after striking a mine 4 miles off Folkestone Light Vessel. The mine was laid by the German submarine UC6.

63. BARON INCHCAPE (I)

ON.139157. 5,603g, 3,582n. 423.5 x 56.0 x 28.7 feet.
T. 3-cyl. (556nhp) by D. Rowan & Co., Glasgow.
1916: Sold, whilst under construction by Russell & Co., Port Glasgow, to James Nourse Ltd., London. *9.1916:* Completed as MEGNA. *1935:* Sold to Atlanticos S.S. Co. Ltd. (Kulukundis Bros. (later Kulukundis Shipping Co. S.A.) managers), Greece and renamed MOUNT ATLAS. *1940:* Sold to Yamashita Kisen K.K., Japan and renamed KUWAYAMA MARU. *21.2.1943:* Torpedoed and sunk off Macassar by the U.S. Submarine THRESHER.

s.s. BARON BERWICK (I) at Swansea *D. Morris, Swansea*

64. BARON BERWICK (I) (1917-1928)

ON.118624. 2,340g, 1,502n. 306.0 x 44.2 x 20.0 feet.
T. 3-cyl. (247nhp) by North Eastern Marine Engineering Co. Ltd., Newcastle.
10.1903: Completed by Craig, Taylor & Co., Stockton as KILDARE for the Kilsyth Shipping Co. Ltd. (Blair, Moffet & Co. managers), Newcastle. *1909:* Management transferred to D. Russell & Co., Leith. *1911:* Sold to Melrose Abbey Shipping Co. Ltd. (F. Jones & Co. managers), Cardiff. *1914:* Renamed NEATH ABBEY by her owners. *1916:* Sold to Dulcia S.S. Co. Ltd. (J.C. Gould & Co. managers), Cardiff and renamed GRELMAY. *1917:* Purchased by the Kelvin Shipping Co. Ltd. and renamed BARON BERWICK. *1928:* Sold to K. Behrsing, Latvia (Connell & Grace Ltd., Newcastle managers) and renamed LIVONIA. *1931:* Sold to J. Salcmans & K. Jansens, Latvia (under same management). *24.12.1931:* Wrecked at Lyserort, whilst on passage from Gdynia to Riga.

s.s. BARON INCHCAPE (II) *Elsam, Mann & Cooper, Liverpool*

65. BARON INCHCAPE (II) (1917-1952)

ON.135731. 7,005g, 5,202n. 425.8 x 56.2 x 33.3 feet.
T. 3-cyl. (379nhp) by J.G. Kincaid & Co. Ltd., Greenock.
9.1917: Completed by Ayrshire Dockyard Co. Ltd., Irvine for the Hogarth Shipping Co. Ltd. *1952:* Sold to Kemal Sadikoglu, Turkey and renamed C. SADIKOGLU. *1959:* Sold to Ticaret Turk Anonim Sti., Turkey and renamed TITAS. *1962:* Sold to Mrs. M. Sadikoglu, Turkey and renamed KAPTAN ASLAN. *12.11.1969:* Mehmet Canakci ve Ortaklari began demolition at Halic.

66. BARON ELCHO (I) (1918-1930)

ON.121259. 4,286g, 2,775n. 376.0 x 49.2 x 19.6 feet.
T. 3-cyl (418nhp) by Clyde S.B. & E. Co. Ltd., Port Glasgow.
9.1905: Completed by William Hamilton & Co. Ltd., Port Glasgow as HYNDFORD for Scottish Shipowners Co. Ltd. (Robertson, Paterson & Co. Ltd. managers), Glasgow. *1918:* Purchased by the Hogarth Shipping Co. Ltd. and renamed BARON ELCHO. *5.1930:* Sold to the West of Scotland Shipbreaking Co., Troon for breaking up.

67. BARON DOUGLAS (II) (1919-1929)

ON.119874. 2,485g, 1,571n. 310.0 x 44.1 x 20.5 feet.
T. 3-cyl. (242nhp) by Blair & Co. Ltd., Stockton.
7.1905: Completed by Ropner & Son, Stockton as GLENMAY for R. Livingstone & Co., West Hartlepool. *1915:* Sold to the Cambo Shipping Co. Ltd. (Morgan & Cadogan Ltd. managers), Cardiff. *1919:* Purchased by the Kelvin Shipping Co. Ltd. and renamed BARON DOUGLAS. *2.1929:* Sold to Kirtatas Bros., Greece and renamed AFROESSA. *6.1940:* Seized by Vichy France at Dakar and renamed SAHARA. *1943:* Retaken at Dakar and renamed AFROESSA. *1944:* Taken over by the Ministry of War Transport for use as a store hulk at Freetown and renamed WOOLWORTH. *1952:* Dismantled.

68. CAMPUS. (1919)

ON.119218. 3054g, 1936n. 325.0 x 47.1 x 13.8 feet..
T. 3-cyl. (275nhp) by Richardsons, Westgarth & Co. Ltd., Hartlepool.
10.1905: Completed by Irvine's Shipbuilding & Dry Docks Co. Ltd., West Hartlepool as NORFOLK RANGE for the Neptune S.N. Co. Ltd. (F. W. Bolam manager), Newcastle. *1910:* Company taken over by Furness, Withy & Co. Ltd., West Hartlepool. *1913:* Sold to the Tempus Shipping Co. Ltd. (W. H. Seager & Co. managers), Cardiff and renamed CAMPUS. *1919:* Purchased by the Kelvin Shipping Co. Ltd., without renaming. *1919:* Sold to St. David's Nav. Co. Ltd. (E. L. & F. P. Williams managers), Cardiff and renamed MARSHAL PLUMER. *1921:* Sold to St. Mary S.S. Co. Ltd. (Williams Bros. (Cardiff) Ltd. managers), Cardiff and renamed BROOKWAY. *1924:* Sold to Awanokuni Kyodo Kisen Kabushiki Kaisha, Japan and renamed TSURUGISAN MARU. *1938:* Name respelt TURUGISAN MARU. *27.10.1942:* Sunk by U.S. air attack off Bougainville.

69. BARON AILSA (II) (1919-1934)

ON.143105. 2,546g, 1,428n. 303.0 x 43.0 x 20.7 feet.
T. 3-cyl. (331 nhp) by Richardsons, Westgarth & Co. Ltd., Hartlepool.
4.1919: Completed by Charles Hill & Sons, Bristol as WAR GUAVA for The Shipping Controller and placed under the management of A. Matthew & Co. *9.1919:* Purchased by the Kelvin Shipping Co. Ltd. and renamed BARON AILSA. *1934:* Sold to A. H. Smith, London. *1935:* Sold to P. G. Callimanopulos, Greece and renamed GRIGORIOS C. II. *20.2.1941:* Sunk by the German warship ADMIRAL SCHEER in the Indian Ocean, S.W. of the Seychelles.

70. BARON GARIOCH (II) (1919-1935)

ON.143317. 2,508g, 1,458n. 303.3 x 43.0 x 20.0 feet.
T. 3-cyl. (217 nhp) by Douglas & Grant Ltd., Kirkcaldy.
1918: Completed by the Forth Shipbuilding & Engineering Co. Ltd., Alloa as WAR MELON for The Shipping Controller and placed under the management of J. Hopper. *10.1919:* Purchased by the Kelvin Shipping Co. Ltd. and renamed BARON GARIOCH. *1935:* Sold to the Guardian Line Ltd. (C. A. Roberts manager), Cardiff and renamed MACGREGOR. *11.6.1938:* Damaged by air attack during the Spanish civil war. *1941:* Sold to Ohlson & Co. Ltd. (Sir. Eric Ohlson, Bart., manager), Hull. *27.2.1942:* Sunk by gunfire from U.156 N.W. of Puerto Rico (position 19.50N. 69.40W. approx.), while on a voyage from the Tyne to Tampa, Fla.

71. BARON SEMPILL (II) (1919-1934)

ON.142771. 2,498g, 1,447n. 303.0 x 43.0 x 20.5 feet.
T. 3-cyl. (331 nhp) by W. Simons & Co. Ltd., Renfrew.
1.1919: Completed By Charles Hill & Sons, Bristol as WAR PLUM for The Shipping Controller (Gillespie & Nicol managers). *11.1919:* Purchased by the Kelvin Shipping Co. Ltd. and renamed BARON SEMPILL. *1934:* Sold to A.H. Smith, London. *1934:* Sold to U.S.S.R. and renamed USSURI. *1959:* Deleted from "Lloyd's Register" owing to lack of current information.

s.s. BARON SEMPILL (II) at Aberdeen, 1923

72. BARON BLANTYRE (II) (1919-1923)
ON.142721. 5,193g, 3,155n. 400.0 x 52.3 x 28.5 feet.
T. 3-cyl. (517 nhp) by the Shipbuilders.
12.1918: Completed by Scotts' Shipbuilding & Engineering Co. Ltd., Greenock as WAR DUCK for The Shipping Controller and placed under the management of H. Hogarth & Sons. *1919:* Purchased by the Hogarth Shipping Co. Ltd. and renamed BARON BLANTYRE. *9.8.1923:* Left Port Natal for Adelaide with a cargo of coal and disappeared.

73. BARON CAWDOR (III) (1920-1926)
ON.143278. 5,864g, 3,677n. 422.5 x 56.2 x 29.6 feet.
T. 3-cyl. (420 nhp) by the Shipbuilders.
1914: Completed by Actien Gesellschaft "Weser", Bremen as NEUMARK for Hamburg-Amerikanische Packetfahrt Aktien Gesellschaft, Germany. *1919:* Surrendered to the U.K. as a prize and managed for The Shipping Controller by J. M. Campbell & Son, Glasgow. *4.11.1920:* Purchased by the Hogarth Shipping Co. Ltd. and renamed BARON CAWDOR. *1926:* Sold to Deutsche Dampfschifffahrts Gesellschaft "Hansa", Germany and renamed EHRENFELS. *1932:* Sold to W. Schuchmann, Germany and renamed WESTSEE. *30.11.1942:* Sunk by Russian shore batteries on the Fischer Peninsula off Petsamofjord after being torpedoed by a Russian submarine.

74. BARON LOVAT (III) (1921-1925)
ON.143079. 6.190g, 3,848n. 470.5 x 61.9 x 25.2 feet.
T. 3-cyl. (703 nhp) by the Shipbuilders.
1916: Completed by J.C. Tecklenborg A.G., Geestemunde as WOLFSBURG for Deutsche Dampfschifffahrts Gesellschaft "Hansa", Germany. *1919:* Surrendered to the U.K. as a prize and managed for The Shipping Controller by Elder, Dempster & Co. Ltd., Liverpool. *30.4.1921:* Purchased by the Hogarth Shipping Co. Ltd. and renamed BARON LOVAT. *1925:* Resold to Deutsche Dampfschifffahrts Gesellschaft "Hansa", Germany and renamed WOLFSBURG. *2.3.1940:* Scuttled North of Iceland, in position 67.50N. 22.45W., to avoid capture by the Royal Navy.

s.s. **BARON LOVAT (III), ex WOLFSBURG**

75. BARON OGILVY (II) (1921-1924).
ON.143366. 5,931g, 3,658n. 451.4 x 58.2 x 30.9 feet.
Quadruple expansion 4-cyl. (500 nhp) by the Shipbuilders.
1918: Completed by Flensburger Schiffsbau Gesellschaft, Flensburg as FORST for Deutsch-Australische Dampfschiffs-Gesellschaft, Germany. *1919:* Surrendered to the U.K. as a prize and managed for The Shipping Controller by G. Dodd & Co., London. *30.4.1921:* Purchased by Hogarth Shipping Co. Ltd. and renamed BARON OGILVY. *1924:* Sold to Roland-Linie A.G., Germany and renamed MURLA. *1925:* Owners became Norddeutscher Lloyd, Germany. *1932:* Sold to U.S.S.R. and renamed MINSK. *1960:* Deleted from "Lloyds Register" owing to lack of current information.

76. BARON VERNON (II) (1922-1924)
ON.135735. 2,603g, 1,507n. 310.0 x 45.0 x 20.7 feet.
T. 3-cyl. (292 nhp) by Richardsons, Westgarth & Co. Ltd., Hartlepool.
1922: Completed by Irvine's Shipbuilding & Dry Docks Co. Ltd., West Hartlepool for the Kelvin Shipping Co. Ltd. She had been launched as DUNMORE HEAD for the Ulster S.S. Co. Ltd., Belfast and was purchased whilst fitting out. *1924:* Sold to Dawson Shipping Co. Ltd. (Dawson Bros. & Rowan managers), Glasgow and renamed DOWANHILL. *1927:* Sold to Cie. des Affrêteurs Francaise, France and renamed MONCEAU. *1929:* Sold to Constants (South Wales) Ltd. (M. Constant manager), Cardiff and renamed HAWKINGE. *12.12.1929:* Wrecked·near Cape Finisterre, whilst on passage from Lisbon to Bilbao in ballast.

s.s. **BARON VERNON (II) at Savona**

s.s. BARON FORBES (I) at Lisbon, 1923

77. BARON FORBES (I) (1922-1953)
ON.143130. 3061g, 1843n. 311.7 x 42.4 x 26.0 feet.
T. 3-cyl. (253 nhp) by Ottensener Maschinenfabrik, Altona.
1915: Completed by Schiffswerft von Henry Koch, Lubeck as HAMBURG for the Oldenburg-Portugiesische Dampfschiffs-Rhederei, Germany. *1919:* Surrendered to Great Britain as a prize and managed for The Shipping Controller by W.A. Young & Co., London. *1920:* Sold to the Byron S.S. Co. Ltd., London and renamed GENERAL NAPIER. *1922:* Purchased by H. Hogarth & Sons and renamed BARON FORBES. *1924:* Registered under the Iberia Shipping Co. Ltd. *16.1.1953:* Arrived at Port Glasgow to be broken up by Smith & Houston Ltd.

s.s. BARON GLENCONNER (I)   *World Ship Photo Library*

28

78. BARON HERRIES (II) (1923-1934)

ON.142569. 2,500g, 1,456n. 303.0 x 43.0 x 20.8 feet
T. 3-cyl. (331 nhp) by Richardsons, Westgarth & Co. Ltd., Hartlepool.
7.1919: Completed by Charles Hill & Sons, Bristol as TREVELYAN for the Hain S. S. Co. Ltd. (E. Hain & Son managers), London, having been laid down as WAR QUINCE for The Shipping Controller. *1923:* Purchased by the Kelvin Shipping Co. Ltd. and renamed BARON HERRIES. *7.1934:* Sold to the Abbey Line Ltd. (Frederick Jones & Sons managers), Cardiff and renamed NEATH ABBEY. *1939:* Sold to Constants (South Wales) Ltd. (M. Constant manager), Cardiff and renamed LYMINGE. *1947:* Sold to Wheelock, Marden & Co. Ltd., London. *1948:* Sold to the San Peh S. N. Co. Ltd., China, renamed TUNG SHAN and registered in the ownership of the Hoong On S. N. Co. Ltd. *15.8.1949:* Bombed and sunk in the Yangtse River, 60 miles from Shanghai, whilst on passage from Shanghai to Pukow.

79. BARON GLENCONNER (I) (1923-1932)

ON.146713. 2,999g, 1,844n. 332.6 x 48.2 x 22.0 feet
T. 3-cyl. (225 nhp) by J.G. Kincaid & Co. Ltd., Greenock.
1923: Completed by Napier & Miller Ltd., Glasgow for the Kelvin Shipping Co. Ltd. *11.1931:* Stranded at Fort Judith. *1932:* Salved and sold to the Osceola S. S. Co. Inc. (C. D. Mallory & Co. Inc. managers), U.S.A. *1933:* Renamed MALTON, same owners. *1935:* Registered under the Maltran S. S. Co. Inc. (same managers). *1937:* Registered under the C. D. Mallory Corporation. *1941:* Taken over by the United States Maritime Commission and renamed TINTAGEL. *1946:* Broken up by the New Market Steel Company, Perth Amboy, demolition being completed by 10.1946.

s.s. BARON ELIBANK (II)

80. BARON ELIBANK(II) (1923-1934)

ON.141938. 2,579g, 1,428n. 303.3 x 43.0 x 20.7 feet.
T. 3-cyl. (265 nhp) by McKie & Baxter, Glasgow
12.1919: Completed by the Ardrossan Dry Dock & Shipbuilding Co. Ltd., Ardrossan as GLASSFORD for the Pennant Shipping Co. Ltd. (Sir John Daniel & Co. Ltd. managers), Cardiff, having been purchased from Mann, MacNeal & Co. Ltd., Glasgow whilst under construction. *1922:* Management taken over by W. E. Hinde & Co., Cardiff. *1923:* Purchased by the Kelvin Shipping Co. Ltd. and renamed BARON ELIBANK. *1934:* Sold to the Good Hope Shipping Co. Ltd. (Walter Vaughan (Cardiff) Ltd. managers), Cardiff and renamed SEVEN SEAS SPRAY. *10.1937:* Seized by Spanish authorities at Santona, but released the following month. *1937:* Sold to the Veronica S. S. Co. Ltd., Cardiff and renamed SEABANK SPRAY. *1938:* Sold to Alfred J. Pope, Cardiff. *1939:* Sold to the Mooringwell S. S. Co. Ltd., Cardiff and later renamed JEANNE M. *2.12.1940:* Torpedoed and sunk by U37 about 250 miles West of Lisbon in position 39.19N. 13.54W. while on a voyage from Cardiff to Lisbon. 7 of her crew were lost.

81. BARON KELVIN (III) (1924-1941)

ON.146714. 3,081g, 1,872n. 332.2 x 48.2 x 22.1 feet.
T. 3-cyl. (225 nhp) by D. Rowan & Co. Ltd., Glasgow.
1924: Completed by Charles Connell & Co. Ltd., Glasgow for the Kelvin Shipping Co. Ltd. *19.10.1941:* Torpedoed and sunk by U206 in position 100° 14 miles from Tarifa. 26 crew lost.

m.v. BARON DALMENY (II) as 'Michael'   *Skyfotos*

82. BARON DALMENY (II) (1924-1937)
ON.146715. 3,536g, 2,215n. 348.7 x 50.0 x 24.0 feet. Motorship.
6-cyl. Two stroke cycle single acting oil engine of 642 nhp., by D. Rowan & Co. Ltd., Greenock, replaced in 1929 by a 6-cyl. four stroke cycle single acting oil engine of 355 nhp by J. G. Kincaid & Co. Ltd., Greenock.
3.1924: Completed by William Hamilton & Co. Ltd., Port Glasgow to their own account but registered under H. Hogarth & Sons who operated the vessel. *1929:* Re-engined. *4.1937:* Sold to Dann's Skibs A/S (Clemeth Dann, manager), Norway and renamed DANIO. *1949:* Sold to D/S Patria A/S II (O. Skjelbred Knudsen manager), Norway. *1950:* Sold to Partrederi Canasta (H. Krohn Brekke manager), Norway and renamed CANASTA. *1952:* Sold to Partenreederi M/S "Michael" (Holsten Reed. G.m.b.H. managers), Germany and renamed MICHAEL. *1956:* Owners became Holsten Reederei Lenth & Co., Germany. *10.1959:* Sold to Eisen & Metall K.G. Lehr & Co., West Germany for breaking up. *2.1960:* Resold to Erich Drechser, West Germany. *5.1960:* Sold back to Eisen & Metall who commenced demolition later that month.

83. BARON WEMYSS (II) (1924-1937)
ON.146716. 2,996g, 1,830n. 332.2 x 48.1 x 21.9 feet.
T. 3-cyl. (225 nhp) by D. Rowan & Co. Ltd., Glasgow.
1924: Completed by Dunlop, Bremner & Co. Ltd., Port Glasgow for the Kelvin Shipping Co. Ltd. *1937:* Sold to A. T. Rosasco, Italy and renamed SANTAROSA. *12.1941:* Seized by U.S.A. at Norfolk, Va, operated by the United States War Shipping Administration, and renamed RAMAPO under the Panamanian flag. *16.2.1942:* Sunk by U.108 North of Bermuda, whilst on passage from Riverport N.S. to New York. All her crew were lost.

84. BARON MURRAY (I) (1924-1938)
ON.146717. 3,103g, 1,840n. 332.6 x 48.3 x 22.0 feet.
T. 3-cyl. (225 nhp) by D. Rowan & Co. Ltd., Glasgow.
1924: Completed by Napier & Miller Ltd., Glasgow for the Kelvin Shipping Co. Ltd. *1938:* Sold to Cia. Carbonifera y de Fundicion Schwager, Chile and renamed QUINENCO. *1951:* Sold to Cia. Maritima Nacional S.A., Chile and renamed SANTIAGO. *29.3.1953* Went aground at Guarello, refloated the following day and declared a constructive total loss. Repaired and returned to service. *27.11.1957:* Went aground at the entrance to Puerto Eden. *3.12.1957:* Refloated. *1958:* Owners became Cia. Maritima Valck & Monckton S.A., Chile. *12.8.1959:* Arrived at Split for breaking up by Brodospas.

85. BARON MACLAY (I) (1924-1957)
ON.146718. 6,317g, 3,870n. 430.4 x 56.3 x 29.1 feet.
T. 3-cyl. (400 nhp) by McKie & Baxter, Glasgow.
11.1924: Completed by the Ayrshire Dockyard Co. Ltd., Irvine for the Hogarth Shipping Co. Ltd. *6.1957:* Sold to "Ave" Soc. di Navigazione S.p.A., Italy and renamed TEBRO. *4.1959:* Sold to United Mineral Trading Co., Panama and renamed BETRO. *1.10.1959:* Arrived at Hirao, Japan for breaking up by Kinoshita & Co.

86. BARON FAIRLIE (II) (1925-1954)
ON.146719. 6,706g, 4,009n. 440.7 x 57.4 x 29.2 feet.
T. 3-cyl. (400 nhp) by McKie & Baxter Ltd., Glasgow.
4.1925: Completed by the Ayrshire Dockyard Co. Ltd., Irvine for the Hogarth Shipping Co. Ltd. *11.1954:* Sold to Mintric Cia. Ltda., Costa Rica and renamed MINTRIC. *1959:* Seized by the Indonesian Government and converted into a naval cadet training ship. Renamed NANUSA.

s.s. BARON FAIRLIE (II)

A. Duncan, Gravesend

87. BARON BELHAVEN (iI) (1925-1957)
ON.146720. 6,591g, 3,921n. 435.2 x 57.3 x 29.6 feet.
T. 3-cyl. (400 nhp) by D. Rowan & Co. Ltd., Glasgow.
6.1925: Completed by Lithgows Ltd., Port Glasgow for the Hogarth Shipping Co. Ltd. *1957:* Sold to United Overseas Marine Corporation, Panama and renamed PACIFIC SKIPPER. *1963:* Sold to Japanese shipbreakers. *4.5.1963:* Demolition commenced at Oppama, Yokosuka.

88. BARON CARNEGIE (1925-1941)
ON.148981. 3,178g, 1,904n. 336.3 x 48.5 x 22.2 feet.
T. 3-cyl. (225 nhp) by D. Rowan & Co. Ltd., Glasgow.
1925: Completed by Dunlop, Bremner & Co. Ltd., Port Glasgow for the Kelvin Shipping Co. Ltd. *11.6.1941:* Torpedoed by aircraft about 15 miles W. of St. David's Head, in position 51.55N. 05.34W and later sank while in tow. 25 of her crew were lost.

89. BARON RUTHVEN (1925-1950)
ON.148982. 3,178g, 1,904n. 336.3 x 48.5 x 22.2 feet.
T. 3-cyl. (225 nhp) by D. Rowan & Co. Ltd., Glasgow.
8.1925: Completed by Dunlop, Bremner & Co. Ltd., Port Glasgow for the Hogarth Shipping Co. Ltd. *6.1950:* Sold to Bremer Schiffahrtskontor Brink & Co. K.G., Germany and renamed INDUSTRIA. *3.1955:* Sold to Johannes Ick, Germany and renamed ILSE. *1962:* Sold to Eisen & Metall A.G. for breaking up. *8.1.1963:* Demolition commenced at Hamburg.

90. BARON NAIRN (1925-1941)
ON.148983. 3.164g, 1,914n. 336.1 x 48.5 x 22.4 feet.
T. 3-cyl. (225 nhp) by J. G. Kincaid & Co. Ltd., Greenock.
1925: Completed by Lithgows Ltd., Port Glasgow for the Kelvin Shipping Co. Ltd. *7.6.1941:* Torpedoed and sunk by U.108 West of Cape Race, in position 47.36N., 39.02W while on a voyage from the Clyde to Nuevitas.

91. BARON GRAHAM (1925-1950)
ON.148984. 3,242g, 1,957n. 336.4 x 48.4 x 22.6 feet.
T. 3-cyl. (225 nhp) by D. Rowan & Co. Ltd., Glasgow.
11.1925: Completed by Napier & Miller Ltd., Glasgow for the Hogarth Shipping Co. Ltd. *1950:* Sold to Schulte & Bruns, Germany and renamed HERMANN SCHULTE. *4.1954:* Sold to Riza ve Aslan Sadikoglu Ortaklari Komandit Sirketi, Turkey and renamed HUSEYIN. *12.1958:* Sold to Ziya Kalkavan Koll. Sti., Turkey and renamed HALIS KALKAVAN. Still in service.

92. BARON LOUDOUN. (1925-1940)
ON.148985. 3,164g, 1,914n. 336.1 x 48.5 x 22.4 feet.
T. 3-cyl. (225 nhp) by J. G. Kincaid & Co. Ltd., Greenock.
1925: Completed by Lithgows Ltd., Port Glasgow for the Kelvin Shipping Co. Ltd, *19.6.1940:* Torpedoed and sunk by U.48 N.W. of Cape Ortegal, in position 45.00N. 11.21W. while on a voyage from Bona to Barrow, 3 crew lost.

s.s. BARON HAIG

93. BARON HAIG (1926-1956)
ON.148986. 3,391g, 2,039n. 342.2 x 48.6 x 22.7 feet.
T. 3-cyl. (225 nhp) by D. Rowan & Co. Ltd., Glasgow.
2.1926: Completed by Ayrshire Dockyard Co. Ltd., Irvine for the Hogarth Shipping Co. Ltd. *1,1956:*
Sold to "Star" Soc. de Nav. S.A., Panama and renamed ESTRELLA. *3.4.1963:* Stranded 2 miles East
of Sile Lighthouse in the Black Sea, whilst on passage from Ilichevsk to Taranto, and was abandoned
by her crew as a total loss.

94. BARON OGILVY (III) (1926-1942)
ON.148988. 3,391g, 2,035n. 342.0 x 48.6 x 22.7 feet.
T. 3-cyl. (225 nhp) by D. Rowan & Co. Ltd., Glasgow.
1926: Completed by Aryshire Dockyard Co. Ltd., Irvine for the Hogarth Shipping Co. Ltd. *29.9.1942:*
Torpedoed and sunk by U.125 S.W. of Cape Palmas, in position 02.30N., 14.30W. 8 crew killed and 3
wounded.

95. BARON LOVAT (IV) (1926-1941)
ON.148989. 3,395g, 2,037n. 342.1 x 48.6 x 22.7 feet.
T. 3-cyl. (225 nhp) by D. Rowan & Co. Ltd., Glasgow.
1926: Completed by Ayrshire Dockyard Co. Ltd., Irvine for the Hogarth Shipping Co. Ltd. *1932:*
Ownership transferred to Hugh Hogarth & Sons. *6.6.1941:* Torpedoed and sunk by the Italian
submarine GUGLIELMO MARCONI S.W. of Cape St. Vincent, in position 35.30N. 11.30W. while on
a voyage from the Tyne to Huelva.

96. BARON TWEEDMOUTH (II) (1927-1951)
ON.148990. 3,357g, 2,023n. 340.3 x 48.7 x 22.7 feet.
T. 3-cyl. (225 nhp) by J.G. Kincaid & Co. Ltd., Greenock.
6.1927: Completed by Lithgows Ltd., Port Glasgow for the Hogarth Shipping Co. Ltd. *1951:* Sold to
Luigi Monta fu Carlo, Italy and renamed MARINERI. *1.1954:* Sold to Liberian Steamship Corporation
RAVALA, Liberia and renamed LORNA. *1968:* Sold to Cia. de Nav. Pinares, Somali Republic. *1974:*
Sold to Brodospas, who began demolition at Split in 3.1974.

97. BARON KINNAIRD (I) (1927-1943)
ON.160121. 3,355g, 2,022n. 340.1 x 48.7 x 22.7 feet.
T. 3-cyl. (225 nhp) by D. Rowan & Co. Ltd., Glasgow.
1927: Completed by Napier & Miller Ltd., Glasgow for the Hogarth Shipping Co. Ltd. *12.3.1943:*
Torpedoed and sunk by U.653 in the North Atlantic, in position 53N. 44W., with the loss of Captain L.
Anderson and all 40 crew. She was on a voyage from Loch Ewe to Macoris.

98. BARON PENTLAND (I) (1927-1941)
ON.160122. 3,410g, 2,045n. 342.1 x 48.6 x 22.8 feet.
T. 3-cyl. (225 nhp) by D. Rowan & Co. Ltd., Glasgow.
1927: Completed by Ayrshire Dockyard Co. Ltd., Irvine for the Kelvin Shipping Co. Ltd. *10.9.1941:*
Torpedoed by U.652 submarine off Cape Farewell, in position 61.15N. 41.05W. 2 crew lost.
19.9.1941: Again torpedoed, by U.372, and sunk.

s.s. BARON SALTOUN

99. BARON SALTOUN (1927-1940)
ON.160123. 3,404g, 2,041n. 342.1 x 48.6 x 22.7 feet.
T. 3-cyl. (240 nhp) by D. Rowan & Co. Ltd., Glasgow.
1927: Completed by the Ayrshire Dockyard Co. Ltd., Irvine for the Iberia Shipping Co. Ltd. *12.6.1940:*
Sank after striking a mine in the Outer Roads, Cherbourg.

100. BARON COCHRANE (1927-1942)
ON.160124. 3,385g, 2,031n. 341.8 x 48.6 x 22.7 feet.
T. 3-cyl. (240nhp) by D. Rowan & Co. Ltd., Glasgow.
1927: Completed by the Ayrshire Dockyard Co. Ltd., Irvine for the Hogarth Shipping Co. Ltd.
28.12.1942: Torpedoed and sunk by U.123 North of the Azores, in position 43.23N., 27.14W. 2 crew
lost.

101. BARON YARBOROUGH (II) (1928—1955)
ON.160125. 3,388g, 2,034n. 341.6 x 48.6 x 22.7 feet.
T. 3-cyl. (240 nhp) by D. Rowan & Co. Ltd., Glasgow.
3.1928: Completed by the Ayrshire Dockyard Co. Ltd., Irvine for the Kelvin Shipping Co. Ltd. *1955:*
Sold to "Algol" Compagnia di Navigazione S.p.A., Italy and renamed ALGOL D. *1956:* Renamed
ALGOL, same owners. *1963:* Owners became Sicula Oceanica S.A., Italy. *19.11.1964:* Arrived at
Spezia for demolition by the Cantieri Navali "Santa Maria".

102. BARON NEWLANDS (1928-1942)
ON.160126. 3,386g, 2,031n. 341.8 x 48.6 x 22.7 feet.
T. 3-cyl. (240 nhp) by D. Rowan & Co. Ltd., Glasgow.
1928: Completed by the Ayrshire Dockyard Co. Ltd., Irvine for the Hogarth Shipping Co. Ltd.
16.3.1942: Torpedoed and sunk by U.68 off the Ivory Coast, in position 04.35N., 08.32W. 18 crew
lost.

103. BARON VERNON (III) (1929-1942)
ON.160127. 3,642g, 2,205n. 350.1 x 50.2 x 23.2 feet.
T. 3-cyl. (249 nhp) by D. & W. Henderson & Co. Ltd., Shipbuilders.
1929: Completed by D. & W. Henderson & Co. Ltd., Glasgow for the Kelvin Shipping Co. Ltd.
30.10.1942: Torpedoed and sunk by U.604 near Madeira, in position 36.06N. 16.59W. while on a
voyage from Freetown to Belfast.

s.s. BARON RAMSAY at Cape Town *World Ship Photo Library*

104. BARON RAMSAY (1929-1959)
ON.160128. 3,650g, 2,211n. 350.0 x 50.2 x 23.2 feet.
T. 3-cyl. (249 nhp) by the Shipbuilders.
7.1929: Completed by D. & W. Henderson & Co. Ltd., Glasgow for the Iberia Shipping Co. Ltd.
1,1959: Sold to the British Iron & Steel Corp. Ltd. for breaking up. *7.9.1959:* Arrived at Port Glasgow
for scrapping by Smith & Houston Ltd.

105. BARON POLWARTH (II) (1929-1937)
ON.160129. 3,661g, 2,211n. 350.9 x 50.1 x 23.2 feet.
T. 3-cyl. (249 nhp) by D. Rowan & Co. Ltd., Glasgow.
1929: Completed by Napier & Miller Ltd., Glasgow for the Hogarth Shipping Co. Ltd. *29.1.1937:*
Grounded on Juan de Nova Reef, Mozambique, whilst on passage from Vizagapatam to Workington
and broke her back. She was abandoned on 6.2.1937.

106. BARON STRANRAER (1929-1950)
ON.160130. 3,668g, 2,220n. 350.7 x 50.2 x 23.3 feet.
T. 3-cyl. (249 nhp) by D. Rowan & Co. Ltd., Glasgow.
10.1929: Completed by Lithgows Ltd., Port Glasgow for the Hogarth Shipping Co. Ltd. *1950:* Sold to
Heinrich Schmidt G.m.b.H., Germany and renamed VENUS. *1957:* Sold to Omeros Shipping Co.,
Liberia and renamed ADELFOTIS II. *1961:* Registered under the Lebanese flag. *20.1.1963:* Whilst on
passage from Middlesbrough to Antwerp in ballast, her steering gear broke down and she put into the
Tyne. After striking the Black Midden Rocks at North Shields, she swung across river and went
aground on the Herd Sands, South Shields where she was abandoned. She became a total loss and
was broken up where she lay by A. Tremble & Sons Ltd., Newcastle.

107. BARON DECHMONT (1929-1943)
ON.161806. 3675g, 2221n. 350.6 x 50.2 x 23.3 feet.
T. 3-cyl. (349 nhp) by J. G. Kincaid & Co. Ltd., Greenock.
1929: Completed by the Ardrossan Dry Dock & Shipbuilding Co. Ltd. for the Hogarth Shipping Co.
Ltd. *3.1.1943:* Torpedoed and sunk by U.507 N.W. of Cape San Roque, Brazil, in position 03.11S.,
38.41W. and 7 of her crew lost, and her Master, Captain D. MacCallum, who was taken aboard the
submarine as a prisoner, was killed when the submarine was bombed and sunk 13.1.1943.

108. BARON BLYTHSWOOD (1929-1940)
ON.161807. 3,668g, 2,219n. 350.7 x 50.2 x 23.3 feet.
T. 3-cyl. (249 nhp) by J. G. Kincaid & Co. Ltd., Greenock.
1929: Completed by Lithgows Ltd., Port Glasgow for the Kelvin Shipping Co. Ltd. *21.9.1940:*
Torpedoed and sunk by U.99 South of Iceland, in position 56N., 23W. (approx.), whilst on passage
from Wabana to Port Talbot, with the loss of Captain J. M. Davies and 33 Crew.

109. BARON NAPIER (II) (1930-1957)
ON.161808. 3,659g, 2,217n. 350.1 x 50.2 x 23.2 feet.
T. 3-cyl. (249 nhp) by the Shipbuilders.
3.1930: Completed by D. & W. Henderson & Co. Ltd., Glasgow for the Hogarth Shipping Co. Ltd.
1957: Sold to Cia. de Vapores Corali Ltda., Liberia and renamed PARCORALI. *17.2.1961:* Stranded
Rosslyn Rock, in position 10.25N., 107.34E., whilst on passage from Bangkok to Japan but refloated
next day. *6.4.1961:* Arrived at Hong Kong. *9.5.1961:* Declared a constructive total loss and sold to
Hong Kong Rolling Mills Ltd., who commenced demolition 23.5.1961.

110. BARON ERSKINE (II) (1930-1942)
ON.161809. 3,657g, 2,216n. 350.0 x 50.2 x 23.2 feet.
T. 3-cyl. (249 nhp) by the Shipbuilders.
1930: Completed by D. & W. Henderson & Co. Ltd., Glasgow for the Kelvin Shipping Co. Ltd.
6.1.1942: Sunk by U.701 North of Rockall, in position 59.15N., 18.30W., whilst on passage from
Tampa to Loch Ewe and Garston. Captain G. S. Cumming and 39 crew lost.

s.s. BARON ARDROSSAN (IV) *W. Ralston, Glasgow*

111. BARON ARDROSSAN (IV) (1932-1940)
ON.161811. 3,896g, 2,334n. 360.9 x 51.7 x 23.4 feet.
T. 3-cyl. (249 nhp) by the Shipbuilders.
1932: Completed by D. & W. Henderson & Co. Ltd., Glasgow for the Hogarth Shipping Co. Ltd.
30.12.1940: Wrecked on Sandray Island, whilst on passage from Calcutta to Hull.

112. BARON DOUGLAS (III) (1932-1957)
ON.161812. 3,899g, 2,342n. 360.8 x 51.7 x 23.4 feet.
T. 3-cyl. (249 nhp) by D. Rowan & Co. Ltd., Glasgow.
10.1932: Completed by Lithgows Ltd., Port Glasgow for Hugh Hogarth & Sons. *1957:* Sold to
"Acrux" Compagnia di Navigazione S.p.A., Italy and renamed ACRUX. *1961:* Sold to Union
Commercial S.S. Co., Lebanon and renamed ARMONIA. *1963:* Renamed HARMONIA, same
owners. *1965:* Sold to Giovanni di Maio, Italy and renamed ANGELO DI MAIO. *1970:* Sold to Cantieri
Navali del Golfo who began demolition at Spezia in 10.1970.

113. BARON DUNMORE (I) (1933-1958)
ON.161813. 3,938g, 2,363n. 365.3 x 51.7 x 23.4 feet.
T. 3-cyl. (249 nhp) by D. Rowan & Co. Ltd., Glasgow.
9.1933: Completed by D. & W. Henderson & Co. Ltd., Glasgow for the Hogarth Shipping Co. Ltd.
5.1958: Sold to the Northern Shipping Co. Inc., Liberia and renamed RHAETIA. *1961:* Sold to
General Ore Carriers Inc., Liberia and renamed ARBON. *1963:* Sold to Irismar S.A., Liberia and
renamed IRIS. *20.9.1971:* Delivered to Brodospas, who began demolition at Split in 11.1971.

114. BARON ELGIN (1933-1958)
ON.161814. 3,942g, 2,364n. 365.4 x 51.7 x 23.4 feet.
T. 3-cyl. (249 nhp) by D. Rowan & Co. Ltd., Glasgow.
10.1933: Completed by D. & W. Henderson & Co. Ltd., Glasgow for the Hogarth Shipping Co. Ltd.
5.1958: Sold to Cia. P. Dannebergs Ltda., Costa Rica and renamed SPIDOLA. *1960:* Transferred to
Nicaraguan registry. *28.3.1970:* Delivered at Bruges to Van Heyghen Freres who began demolition
31.3.1970.

115. BARON CAWDOR (IV) (1935-1959)
ON.161815. 3,638g, 2,132n. 387.1 x 53.2 x 22.5 feet.
T. 3-cyl. (250 nhp) by the Shipbuilders.
1.1935: Completed by D. & W. Henderson & Co. Ltd., Glasgow for the Hogarth Shipping Co. Ltd.
12.1959: Sold to Eisenberg Ltda, Goa for breaking up and resold to Japanese shipbreakers, arriving at
Hirao *17.3.1960.*

s.s. BARON RENFREW (II)

116. BARON RENFREW (II) (1935-1961)
ON.163841. 3,635g, 2,130n. 387.0 x 53.2 x 22.5 feet.
T. 3-cyl. (250 nhp) by the Shipbuilders.
3.1935: Completed by D. & W. Henderson & Co. Ltd., Glasgow for the Kelvin Shipping Co. Ltd.
1961: Sold to Avlis Shipping Co. S.A., Greece and renamed ADAMASTOS. *1967:* Transferred to
Avlis Shipping Co. Special S.A., Greece. *1970:* Sold to Despina Cia. Mar., S.A., Greece, and
renamed DESPINA A. *1971:* Owners became Despina A Shipping Co., S.A., Greece. *1973:* Sold to
Tuber Celik Sanayii A.S., to whom she was delivered at Istanbul *11.5.1973*. *15.8.1973:* Demolition
began at the Golden Horn.

117. BARON AILSA (III) (1936-1940)
ON.163843. 3,656g, 2,148n. 386.4 x 53.2 x 22.5 feet.
T. 3-cyl. (250 nhp) by D. Rowan & Co. Ltd., Glasgow.
1936: Completed by Lithgows Ltd., Port Glasgow for the Kelvin Shipping Co. Ltd. *17.2.1940:* Sank
after striking a mine N.W. of Cromer, in position 53.17N., 01.12E. Two crew, including Captain G. R.
Logan, lost.

s.s. BARON JEDBURGH (II)

118. BARON JEDBURGH (II) (1936-1945)
ON.163844. 3,656g, 2,148n. 386.4 x 53.2 x 22.5 feet.
T. 3-cyl. (250 nhp) by D. Rowan & Co. Ltd., Glasgow.
1936: Completed by Lithgows Ltd., Port Glasgow for the Hogarth Shipping Co. Ltd. *10.3.1945:*
Torpedoed and sunk by U.532 N.E. of Bahia, in position 10.02S., 25.00W. while on a voyage from
Trinidad to Table Bay. All but one of her crew were saved. Of the two lifeboats one, under the
command of Capt. E. A. Brown, reached the Brazilian coast two weeks after the torpedoing. The
occupants of the other boat were picked up by a Union Castle Ship.

s.s. BARON ELPHINSTONE   *Skyfotos*

119. BARON ELPHINSTONE (1937-1959)
ON.163845. 4,635g, 2,692n. 417.1 x 58.2 x 24.1 feet.
T. 3-cyl. (250 nhp) by G. Clark (1936) Ltd., Sunderland.
10.1937: Completed by Sir James Laing & Sons Ltd., Sunderland for the Hogarth Shipping Co. Ltd.
3.1959: Sold to Aristides S.S. Co. S.A., Panama (for a time managed by Rallis Shipping Co. Ltd.) and
renamed ARISTIDES. *30.7.1971:* Arrived at Santander and on *4.8.1971* delivered to Recuperaciones
Submarinas S.A. who began demolition *10.8.1971.*

120. BARON MINTO (II) (1937-1940)
ON.163846. 4,637g, 2,693n. 417.1 x 58.2 x 24.1 feet.
T. 3-cyl. (250 nhp) by G. Clark (1936) Ltd., Sunderland.
1937: Completed by Sir James Laing & Sons Ltd., Sunderland for the Hogarth Shipping Co. Ltd.
30.10.1940: Wrecked in Strathbeg Bay, near Rattray Head, whilst on passage from Texas City to Hull.
14.2.1941: Further damaged by air attack. *9.5.1941:* Declared a constructive total loss.

121. BARON SEMPLE (1939-1943)
ON.163847. 4,573g, 2,670n. 416.1 x 58.2 x 24.6 feet.
T. 3-cyl. (250 nhp) by D. Rowan & Co. Ltd., Glasgow.
1939: Completed by Charles Connell & Co. Ltd., Glasgow for the Kelvin Shipping Co. Ltd. *2.11. 1943:*
Sunk by U.848 N.W. of Ascension Island, in position 05.S. 21W., whilst on passage from Rio de
Janeiro to Freetown and the U.K. She had left Rio de Janeiro *25.10.1943* with a crew of 62, with
Captain Philip J. Carnie in command. All were lost.

122. BARON SCOTT (1940-1961)
ON.163848. 4,574g, 2.660n. 415.7 x 56.4 x 24.3 feet.
T. 3-cyl. (258 nhp) by D. Rowan & Co. Ltd., Glasgow.
1.1940: Completed by Lithgows Ltd., Port Glasgow for the Hogarth Shipping Co. Ltd. *2.1961:* Sold to
Aristides S.S. Co. S.A. (Rallis Shipping Co. Ltd. managers), Panama and renamed CISSOULA.
1964: Sold to F. A. Theodorides (Aristides S.S. Co. S.A. managers), Greece. *1969:* Sold to the China
National Machinery Import and Export Corporation and handed over *24.9.1969* to the shipbreakers at
Hsinkang.

s.s. BARON HERRIES (III)   *Skyfotos*

123. BARON HERRIES (III) (1940-1960)
ON.163849. 4,574g, 2,660n. 415.7 x 56.4 x 24.3 feet.
T. 3-cyl. (258 nhp) by D. Rowan & Co. Ltd., Glasgow.
2.1940: Completed by Lithgows Ltd., Port Glasgow for the Kelvin Shipping Co. Ltd. *10.1960:* Sold to Avlis Shipping Co. S.A., Greece and renamed ATHOS II. *16.3.1962:* Went aground on Hairsis Island, at the entrance to the Bosphorus, whilst on passage from Constantza to Antwerp. *6.1962:* Wreck sold to Ibrahim Kalkavan who commenced demolition *26.6.1962* at Riva Deresi.

s.s. BARON MURRAY (II)   *Skyfotos*

124. BARON MURRAY (II) (1946-1959)
ON.166215. 7,031g, 4,777n. 431.3 x 56.3 x 35.2 feet.
T. 3-cyl. (510 nhp) by North Eastern Marine Engineering Co. (1938) Ltd., Sunderland.
8.1942: Completed by the Caledon Shipbuilding & Engineering Co. Ltd., Dundee as EMPIRE ARCHER for the Ministry of War Transport (Raeburn & Verel Ltd. Glasgow, managers). *1946:* Management transferred to H. Hogarth & Sons. *1946:* Purchased by the Kelvin Shipping Co. Ltd. and renamed BARON MURRAY. *3.1959:* Sold to Cathay Shipping Corporation Ltd., Panama and renamed CATHAY. *24.7.1963:* Arrived at Yokosuka, Japan for breaking up.

125. BARON GEDDES (1946-1959)
ON.168965. 7,049g, 4.941n. 431.5 x 56.2 x 35.2 feet.
T. 3-cyl. (510 nhp) by Central Marine Engine Works, West Hartlepool.
11.1943: Completed by William Gray & Co. Ltd., West Hartlepool as EMPIRE PLOUGHMAN for the Ministry of War Transport (H. Hogarth & Sons managers). *5.1946:* Purchased by the Hogarth Shipping Co. Ltd. and renamed BARON GEDDES. *11.1959:* Sold to Paulins Rederi A/B (later A/B Paulin Chartering O/Y & Co.), Finland and renamed JYTTE PAULIN. *1963:* Owners restyled: A/B Paulin Chartering O/Y & Co. Kommandiittiyhtio/Kommanditbolag. *1968:* Sold to the China National Machinery Import & Export Corporation and arrived at Shanghai prior to *22.10.1968* for breaking up. *See also Managed Ships, page 53.*

126. BARON ELCHO (II) (1946-1955)
ON.168948. 2,865g, 1,687n. 315.4 x 46.5 x 23.0 feet.
T. 3-cyl. (269 nhp) by Central Marine Engine Works, West Hartlepool.
12.1942: Completed by William Gray & Co. Ltd., West Hartlepool as EMPIRE LORENZO for the Ministry of War Transport (Dover Navigation Co. Ltd. managers). *1946:* Purchased by the Hogarth Shipping Co. Ltd. and renamed BARON ELCHO. *1955:* Sold to Compania Maritima Ircar S.A., Liberia and renamed KISMET II. *25.11.1955:* Stranded on Cape Breton Island, whilst on passage from Philadelphia to Summerside, and became a total loss.

s.s. BARON ELIBANK (III)   *Skyfotos*

127. BARON ELIBANK (III) (1946-1959)
ON.168964. 2,905g, 1,641n. 315.4 x 46.5 x 23.0 feet.
T. 3-cyl. (281 nhp) by Central Marine Engine Works, West Hartlepool.
11.1943: Completed by William Gray & Co. Ltd., West Hartlepool as EMPIRE RANSOM for the Ministry of War Transport (H. Hogarth & Sons managers). *8.1946:* Purchased by the Kelvin Shipping Co. Ltd. and renamed BARON ELIBANK. *11.1959:* Sold to Empros Shipping Co. Ltd., Greece and renamed ARMENISTIS. *1966:* Transferred to Empros Shipping Lines Co. Special S.A., Greece. *1971:* Sold to Jos. Boel et fils, to whom she was delivered *6.7.1971* and who began work at Temse in *7.1971.*

128. BARON AILSA (IV) (1946-1955)
ON.180068. 2,905g, 1,641n. 315.4 x 46.5 x 23.0 feet.
T. 3-cyl. (281 nhp) by Central Marine Engine Works, West Hartlepool.
1.1944: Completed by William Gray & Co. Ltd., West Hartlepool as EMPIRE HARCOURT for the Ministry of War Transport (H. Hogarth & Sons managers). *10.1946:* Purchased by the Kelvin Shipping Co. Ltd. and renamed BARON AILSA. *1955:* Sold to Wm. H. Muller & Co. (later: Wm. H.

Muller & Co.'s Transport Maatschappij N.V.), Netherlands and renamed IBERIA. *1962:* Sold to Tankers Finance Corp., Greece and renamed CYCLADIKI DOXA. *1964:* Sold to Cia. Maritima Sarita S.A., Greece and renamed MOUNT SINAI. *10.4.1972:* Demolition commenced at Perama by S. Kyriazis, G. Georgopoulos and D. Politis.
See also Managed Ships, page 54.

Dimensions from here on are length overall x beam x draft at summer deadweight.

m.v. BARON KILMARNOCK   *Skyfotos*

129. BARON KILMARNOCK (1953-1957)
ON.180206. 11,810g, 6,663n. 547'0" x 71'4" x 30'0½". Motor Tanker.
6-cyl. 2 S.C.S.A. oil engine by J.G. Kincaid & Co. Ltd., Greenock.
7.1953: Completed by Caledon Shipbuilding & Engineering Co. Ltd., Dundee for Hogarth Shipping Co. Ltd. and Kelvin Shipping Co. Ltd. *4.1957:* Sold to Det Bergenske Dampskibsselskab, Norway and renamed SPICA. *1966:* Sold to San Antonio S.S. Co. S.A. (John Manners & Co. Ltd. managers), Panama and renamed EASTLAND TRADER. *1966:* Converted into a bulk carrier of 11,056g and renamed SAN ANTONIO, same owners. *1973:* Sold to Lavender Maritime Co. Ltd. Panama and renamed LAVENDER. Still in service.

130. BARON INVERCLYDE (1954-1963)
ON.180207. 5,479g, 2,896n. 456'7" x 57' 6" x 25' 9".
T. 3-cyl. with low pressure steam turbine by the Shipbuilders.
1.1954: Completed by John Readhead & Sons Ltd., South Shields for the Kelvin Shipping Co. Ltd. *1963:* Sold to Medship Corporation, Liberia and renamed JOHN MARIS. *1969:* Sold to Marine Express Transport Corporation, Liberia and renamed SAINT JOHN. *1970:* Sold to Metropolitan Shipping Co. Ltd., Cyprus and renamed GIANNIS. *19.6.1972:* Arrived at Bilbao to be scrapped by Hierros Arbulu, who began work in *11.1972.*

40

s.s. BARON ARDROSSAN (V)

131. BARON ARDROSSAN (V) (1954-1966)
ON.180208. 5,254g, 2,649n. 436'7'' x 57'2'' x 25'5¼''.
T. 3-cyl. with L.P. Turbine by North Eastern Marine Engineering Co. (1938) Ltd., Sunderland.
7.1954: Completed by William Pickersgill & Sons Ltd., Sunderland for the Hogarth Shipping Co. Ltd.
1966: Sold to Empros Lines Shipping Co. Special S.A., Greece and renamed ALIAKMON. Still in service.

132. BARON GLENCONNER (II) (1955-1963)
ON.180209. 5,468g, 2,789n. 461'3'' x 58'3'' x 25'3½''.
T. 3-cyl. with L.P. turbine by J.G. Kincaid & Co. Ltd., Greenock.
9.1955: Completed by Caledon Shipbuilding & Engineering Co. Ltd., Dundee for the Kelvin Shipping Co. Ltd. *1963:* Sold to Ilissus Marine Corp., Liberia and renamed ZITA. *1965:* Sold to Taiwan International Line Ltd., Taiwan China and renamed KUO YANG. *1968:* Sold to Hai Sang S. S. Co., Taiwan & renamed CONVOY PIONEER. *1969:* Sold to Amerworld Navigation Corp, Liberia and renamed AMWORLD. *3.3.1973:* Tung Ho Steel Enterprise Co., Ltd. began demolition at Kaohsiung.

133. BARON OGILVY (IV) (1956-1963)
ON.180210. 5,471g, 2,800n. 456'7'' x 57'6'' x 25'9''.
T. 3-cyl. with L.P. turbine by the Shipbuilders.
7.1956: Completed by John Readhead & Sons Ltd., South Shields for the Hogarth Shipping Co. Ltd. *1963:* Sold to Comercio Cia. Nav. S.A., Liberia and renamed ROMEO. *1967:* Sold to the Santa Anastassia Cia. Nav. S.A., Greece and renamed AGHIA ANASTASIA. *1.9.1969:* Abandoned by her crew in position 32.8S, 75.31E. after developing leaks while in the Indian Ocean during a voyage from Port Pirie to the Bristol Channel with concentrates. She was sighted *6.9.1969* still afloat in 32.08S, 74.07E, but thereafter disappeared.

134. BARON INCHCAPE (III) (1956-1963)
ON.180211. 5,490g, 2,849n. 461'6'' x 58'3'' x 25' 4½''.
T. 3-cyl. with L.P. turbine by J. G. Kincaid & Co. Ltd., Greenock.
9.1956: Completed by Lithgows Ltd., Port Glasgow for the Hogarth Shipping Co. Ltd. *1963:* Sold to the Naxos Shipping Corporation, Liberia and renamed MARIA VOYAZIDES. *1965:* Sold to Afro-Asia Shipping Co. Ltd., Liberia and renamed AFROSIA. *1968:* Sold to the Indonesian Navy. *1970:* Sold to Prompt Shipping Corp, Liberia and renamed PRINCESS VERNA. *1972:* Sold to Eduardo M. Cojuangco, Jr (Northern Carriers Inc, managers) Philippine Islands and renamed MARGARITA. *1973:* Sold to Ta Fah Marine Co. S.A., Panama and renamed FOK SAN. *1975:* Sold to Chou's Iron & Steel Industrial Co., who began demolition at Hualien *18.7.1975.*

135. BARON BERWICK (II) (1956-1965)
ON.180212. 5,471g, 2,800n. 456'7'' x 57'6'' x 25'9''.
T. 3-cyl. with L.P. turbine by the Shipbuilders.
10.1956: Completed by John Readhead & Sons, Ltd., South Shields for the Kelvin Shipping Co., Ltd. *1965:* Sold to the Maureen Corporation, Haiti, and renamed FILTRIC. *1966:* Transferred to Greek registry. *12.1.1970:* Abandoned 5 miles south of Cape Finisterre in a position 42.42.N, 9.20W. after her cargo had shifted during a voyage from Copenhagen to Alexandria, and went aground near Cape Finisterre the following day.

s.s. BARON BERWICK (II)   *Skyfotos*

136. BARON JEDBURGH (III) (1958-1967)
ON.180213. 8,337g, 4,687n. 461'8" x 59'9" x 28'11".
4-cyl. 2 S.C.S.A. oil engine by Hawthorn Leslie (Engineers) Ltd., Newcastle.
7.1958: Completed by John Readhead & Sons Ltd., South Shields for the Hogarth Shipping Co. Ltd.
1966: Registered under H. Hogarth & Sons Ltd. *1967:* Sold to Intercontinental Maritime Ltd., Liberia
and renamed EVIE G. CHIMPLES. *1972:* Transferred to Greek registry. Still in service.

137. BARON GARIOCH (III) (1958-1968)
ON.180214. 8,337g, 4,687n. 461'8" x 59'9" x 28'10¾".
4-cyl. 2 S.C.S.A. oil engine by Hawthorn Leslie (Engineers) Ltd., Newcastle.
10.1958: Completed by John Readhead & Sons Ltd., South Shields for the Kelvin Shipping Co. Ltd.
1965: Sold to the Hogarth Shipping Co. Ltd. *1966:* Registered under H. Hogarth & Sons Ltd. *1968:*
Sold to the Bordagain Shipping Co. Ltd., Liberia and renamed BORDAGAIN. *1976:* Sold to Greek
interests and renamed ERINI PETRA. Still in service.

138. BARON KINNAIRD (II) (1958-1968)
ON.180215. 8,067g, 4,490n, 465'1" x 59'9" x 28'6¼".
4-cyl. 2 S.C.S.A. oil engine by William Doxford & Sons (Engineers) Ltd., Sunderland.
11.1958: Completed by Austin & Pickersgill Ltd., Sunderland for the Hogarth Shipping Co. Ltd. *1966:*
Registered under H. Hogarth & Sons Ltd. *1968:* Sold to the Artagan Shipping Co. Ltd, Liberia and
renamed ARTIBA. *1976:* Sold to Palmist Shipping Corp., Greece and renamed PALMIS. Still in
service.

139. BARON MINTO (III) (1959-1967)
ON.181361. 7,801g, 4377n, 450'0" x 59'8" x 28'6¼".
4-cyl. 2 S.C.S.A. oil engine by William Doxford & Sons (Engineers) Ltd., Sunderland.
2.1959: Completed by Sir James Laing & Sons Ltd., Sunderland for the Hogarth Shipping Co. Ltd.
1966: Registered under H. Hogarth & Sons Ltd. *1967:* Sold to Astro Dichoso Cia. Nav. S.A., Greece
and renamed DIRPHYS II. Still in service.

140. BARON PENTLAND (II) (1959-1968)
ON.181362. 8,067g, 4,490n, 465'1" x 59'9" x 28'6¼".
4-cyl. 2 S.C.S.A. oil engine by Austin & Pickersgill Ltd., Newcastle.
3.1959: Completed by Austin & Pickersgill Ltd., Sunderland for the Kelvin Shipping Co. Ltd. *1965:*
Sold to the Hogarth Shipping Co. Ltd. *1966:* Registered under H. Hogarth & Sons Ltd. *1968:* Sold to
Rio Pardo Cia. Nav. S.A., Greece and renamed AGHIOS NICOLAOS. Still in service.

141. BARON MACLAY (II) (1959-1968)
ON.181363. 8,067g, 4,490n, 465'1" x 59'9" x 28'6¼".
4-cyl. 2 S.C.S.A. oil engine by North Eastern Marine Engineering Co. Ltd., Newcastle.
12.1959: Completed by Austin & Pickersgill Ltd., Sunderland for the Hogarth Shipping Co. Ltd. *1966:*
Registered under H. Hogarth & Sons Ltd. *1968:* Sold to the Artagan Shipping Co Ltd. (Ramon de la
Sota Jr., Manager) Liberia and renamed ARTAGAN. Still in service.

m.v. BARON MACLAY (II) *Skyfotos*

142. BARON BELHAVEN (III) (1960-1967)
ON.181364. 8,337g, 4,687n. 461'8'' x 59'9'' x 28'10¾''.
4-cyl. 2 S.C.S.A. oil engine by Hawthorn Leslie (Engineers) Ltd., Newcastle.
1.1960: Completed by John Readhead & Sons Ltd., South Shields for the Hogarth Shipping Co. Ltd.
1966: Registered under H. Hogarth & Sons Ltd. *1967:* Sold to the Evie Navigation Co. Ltd., Liberia
and renamed GLOBAL TRADER. *1972:* Transferred to Greek registry. Still in service.

143. BARON WEMYSS (III) (1960-1968)
ON.181365. 8,067g, 4,490n. 465'1'' x 59'9'' x 28'6½''.
4-cyl. 2 S.C.S.A. oil engine by North Eastern Marine Engineering Co. Ltd., Newcastle.
2.1960: Completed by Austin & Pickersgill Ltd., Sunderland for the Kelvin Shipping Co. Ltd. *1965:*
Sold to the Hogarth Shipping Co. Ltd. *1966:* Registered under H. Hogarth & Sons Ltd. *1968:* Sold to
the Bordagain Shipping Co. Ltd., Liberia and renamed BORDABARRI. Still in service.

144. BARON INVERFORTH (1965-1969)
ON.181367. 18,319g, 12,000n, 617'0'' x 82'3'' x 35'7½''. Bulk Carrier.
4-cyl. 2 S.C.S.A. oil engine by G. Clark & N.E.M. Ltd., Sunderland.
12.1965: Completed by Austin & Pickersgill Ltd., Sunderland for the Hogarth Shipping Co. Ltd. *1966:*
Registered under H. Hogarth & Sons Ltd. *1969:* Sold to the Paramount Carriers Corporation, Liberia,
and renamed MARGIO. Still in service.

m.v. BARON INVERFORTH *Turners, Newcastle-on-Tyne*

m.v. BARON FORBES (II)

145. BARON FORBES (II) (1967-1973)
ON.181369. 12,649g, 6,925n. 530' 0'' x 71' 3'' x 31' 9¾''. Bulk Carrier.
6-cyl. 2 S.C.S.A. Sulzer oil engine by Marinens Hovedverft, Horten.
10.1967: Completed by Haugesund Mek. Verksted A/S, Haugesund for H. Hogarth & Sons Ltd.
1973: Sold to Seven Seas Transportation Ltd., India and renamed SATYA SOHAN. Still in service.

146. BARON CAWDOR (V) (1968-1975)
ON.181370. 13,580g, 7,654n. 527' 9'' (including bulbous bow) x 75' 2'' x 31' 11½''. Bulk Carrier.
6-cyl. 2 S.C.S.A. Sulzer oil engine by the Shipbuilders.
3.1968: Completed by Marinens Hovedverft, Horten for H. Hogarth & Sons Ltd. *1975:* Sold to the
Australian Shipping Commission, Australia and *later in 1975* renamed STIRLING RANGE. Still in
service.

m.v. BARON CAWDOR (V)

m.v. BARON DUNMORE (II)   *Skyfotos*

147. BARON DUNMORE (II) (1968-   )
ON.335583. 12,660g, 6,914n, 19,958d. 530'0'' (including bulbous bow) x 71'3'' x 31'9¾''. Bulk Carrier.
6-cyl. 2 S.C.S.A. Sulzer oil engine by Marinens Hovedverft, Horten.
12.1968: Completed by Haugesund Mek. Verksted A/S, Haugesund, for H. Hogarth & Sons, Ltd. In the present fleet.

148. BARON RENFREW (III) (1970-   )
ON.335585. 13,544g, 8,080n, 22,200d. 527'9'' (inc. bulbous bow) x 75'2'' x 32'1''. Bulk Carrier.
Two 12-cyl. 2 S.C.S.A. oil engines by English Electric Diesels, Ltd., Ruston Division, Lincoln, geared to a single screw shaft, replaced in 1973 by two 9-cyl. 4 S.C.S.A. oil engines by Stork-Werkspoor Diesel, Amsterdam.
4.1970: Completed by A/S Horten Verft, Horten for H. Hogarth & Sons Ltd. *5.1971:* Port engine replaced. *8.1973:* Re-engined by Amsterdamsche Droogdok Maatschappij, Amsterdam with two Stork-Werkspoor Diesel engines. In the present fleet.

149. BARON ARDROSSAN (VI) (1970-   )
ON.335586. 14,508g, 9,632n, 23,680d. 534'4'' (inc. bulbous bow) x 75'2'' x 34'2''. Bulk Carrier.
Two 12-cyl. 2 S.C.S.A. oil engines by English Electric Diesels, Ltd., Ruston Division, Lincoln, geared to a single screw shaft, replaced in 1973 by two 12-cyl. 4 S.C.S.A. oil engines by Stork-Werkspoor Diesel, Amsterdam.
10.1970: Completed by Haugesund Mek. Verksted A/S, Haugesund, for H. Hogarth & Sons, Ltd. *12.1973:* Re-engined by Amsterdamsche Droogdok Maatschappij, Amsterdam with two Stork-Werkspoor Diesel engines. In the present fleet.

150. BARON BELHAVEN (IV) (1971-   )
ON.335587. 14,885g, 8,802n, 23,340d. 542'0'' (inc. bulbous bow) x 75'2'' x 33'7''. Bulk Carrier.
5-cyl. 2 S.C.S.A. Sulzer oil engines by A/S Horten Verft, Horten.
3.1971: Completed by Kaldnes Mek. Verksted, Tonsberg, for H. Hogarth & Sons Ltd. In the present fleet.

151. BARON INCHCAPE (IV) (1971-   )
ON.335588. 14,651g, 9,896n, 23,700d. 534'4'' (inc. bulbous bow) x 75'3'' x 34'2''. Bulk Carrier.
Two 12-cyl. 2 S.C.S.A. oil engines by Ruston Paxman Diesels, Ltd., Lincoln, geared to a single screw shaft, replaced in 1974 by two 12-cyl 4 S.C.S.A. oil engines by Stork-Werkspoor Diesel, Amsterdam.
5.1971: Completed by Haugesund Mek. Verksted A/S, Haugesund, for H. Hogarth & Sons, Ltd., *3.1974:* Re-engined by Amsterdamsche Droogdok Maatschappij, Amsterdam with two Stork-Werkspoor Diesel engines. In the present fleet.

m.v. BARON MACLAY (III)

152. BARON MACLAY (III) (1971-   )
ON.335589. 13,443g, 7,842n, 21,950d. 522' 4'' (inc. bulbous bow) x 75' 2'' x 32' 0½''. Bulk Carrier.
5-cyl. 2 S.C.S.A. Sulzer oil engines by the shipbuilders.
12.1971: Completed by A/S Horten Verft, Horten, for H. Hogarth & Sons, Ltd. In the present fleet.

153. BARON WEMYSS (IV) (1972-   )
ON.335590. 14,651g, 10,051n, 23,710d. 534' 4'' (inc. bulbous bow) x 75' 2'' x 34' 1½''. Bulk Carrier.
Two 12-cyl. 2 S.C.S.A. oil engines by Ruston Paxman Diesels, Ltd., Lincoln, geared to a single screw
shaft, replaced in 1974 by two 12-cyl.4S C.S.A. oil engines by Stork-Werkspoor Diesel, Amsterdam.
10.1972: Completed by Haugesund Mek. Verksted A/S, Haugesund, for H. Hogarth & Sons, Ltd.
9.1974: Re-engined by Amsterdamsche Droogdok Maatschappij, Amsterdam with two Stork-
Werkspoor Diesel engines. In the present fleet.

m.v. BARON WEMYSS (IV)

BARON NAPIER at Scotstoun, 13th June, 1976 *George Gardner*

154. BARON NAPIER (III) (1976-)
ON.364278. 16,646g, 9,782n, 26,930d. 574' 6'' (inc. bulbous bow) x 83' 6'' x 33' 4''. Bulk Carrier.
6-cyl. 2 S.C.S.A. Burmeister & Wain type oil engine by Harland & Wolff Ltd., Belfast.
6.1976: Completed by Govan Shipbuilders Ltd., Glasgow. In the present fleet.

BARON PENTLAND returning from trials, 16th June, 1976 *George Gardner*

155. BARON PENTLAND (III) (1976-)
ON.364279. 16,844g, 9,931, 26,814d. 574' 6'' (inc. bulbous bow) x 83' 6'' x 33' 4''. Bulk Carrier.
6-cyl. 2 S.C.S.A. Burmeister & Wain type oil engine by Harland & Wolff Ltd., Belfast.
6.1976: Completed by Govan Shipbuilders Ltd., Glasgow. In the present fleet.

156.
32,000d. 587' 0'' (inc. bulbous bow) x 88' 6'' x 48' 6''. Bulk Carrier.
Burmeister & Wain type oil engines.
20.8.1975: Ordered from Mitsui Shipbuilding & Engineering Co. Ltd., Chiba, Japan, to be launched in 1.1977 and delivered in 4.1977. To be named BARON MURRAY.

SHIPS MANAGED DURING
THE TWO WORLD WARS

M1. WAR DRAKE (1918)
ON.142618. 5,183g, 3,160n. 400.6 x 52.3 x 28.5 feet.
T. 3-cyl. by the Shipbuilders.
8.1918: Completed by D. & W. Henderson & Co. Ltd., Glasgow for The Shipping Controller and placed under Hogarth management. *1918:* Sold to the Sefton S.S. Co. Ltd. (H. E. Moss & Co. managers), Liverpool and renamed MOUNT EVEREST. *1923:* Sold to Société Générale de Transports Maritimes à Vapeur, France and renamed MONT EVEREST. *11.1942:* Taken over by U.S.A. at New Orleans. Operated by the United States War Shipping Administration under the Panamanian flag. *1945:* Returned to her former French owners. *1953:* Sold to Compania Armadora San Francisco, Panama and renamed LAGOS ERIE. *1959:* Sold to Mitsubishi Shoji Kaisha for scrapping. *13.2.1959:* Arrived at Tokyo, to be broken up by Amakaso Sangyo.

M2. WAR DUCK (1918-1919) See BARON BLANTYRE (No. 72)

M3. SOLFELS (1919-1920)
ON.143102. 5,821g, 3,641n. 419.7 x 56.1 x 29.7 feet.
T. 3-cyl. by the Shipbuilders.
5.1913: Completed by J. C. Tecklenborg A.G., Geestemunde for Deutsche Dampfschifffahrts-Gesellschaft 'Hansa', Germany. *1919:* Taken as a prize by Great Britain and managed for The Shipping Controller by H. Hogarth & Sons. *1920:* Sold to the Lancashire Shipping Co. Ltd. (J. Chambers & Co. managers), Liverpool and renamed BOWES CASTLE. *1932:* Sold to Achille Lauro, Italy and renamed ANGELINA LAURO. *6.1940:* Seized by Great Britain at Liverpool. Taken over by the Ministry of Shipping (later Ministry of War Transport), renamed EMPIRE ADVOCATE and put under management of Galbraith, Pembroke & Co. Ltd. *16.2.1945:* Arrived at Bo'ness for demolition by P. & W. MacLellan Ltd.

M4. WEISSENFELDE (1919-1920)
ON.143198. 3,926g, 2,522n. 358.0 x 46.1 x 19.5 feet.
Q. 4-cyl. by the Shipbuilders.
6.1899: Completed by Wigham Richardson & Co., Newcastle as WEISSENFELS for Deutsche Dampfschifffahrts-Gesellschaft 'Hansa', Germany. *3.1914:* Sold to D. Fuhrmann, Nissle & Gunther Nachf., Germany and renamed WEISSENFELDE. *1919:* Taken as a prize by Great Britain and managed for The Shipping Controller by H. Hogarth & Sons. *1920:* Allocated to Belgium and managed for the Belgian Government by S. A. Asmar. *1922:* Sold to Ch. de Cort and F. Verschueren, Belgium. *1922:* Sold to W. Schuchmann, Germany and renamed OSTSEE. *21.5.1927:* Stranded at Point Ceres, whilst on passage from Rotterdam to Venice. Refloated and sold to be broken up at Bilbao.

M5. WINFRIED (1919-1920)
ON.143333. 5,271g, 3,296n. 409.0 x 55.1 x 28.4 feet.
Q. 4-cyl. by the Shipbuilders.
4.1911: Completed by J. Frerichs & Co. A.G., Einswarden for Hamburg Bremer Africa Linie A.G., Germany. *1919:* Taken as a prize by Great Britain and managed for The Shipping Controller by H. Hogarth & Sons. *20.12.1920:* Purchased by the St. Just S.S. Co. Ltd. (W.R. Smith & Sons managers), Cardiff and renamed SIAM CITY. *1927:* Sold to Jugoslavensko-Amerikanska Plovidba, Jugoslavia and renamed GUNDULIC. *1928:* Owners restyled: Jugoslavenski-Lloyd d.d. *19.3.1934:* Wrecked at Puerto Bueno, Smyth Channel, Chile whilst on passage from Rosario to Coronel. *1944:* Bought by the Chilean Navy, refloated and taken in tow for Talcahuano for repairs. *1945:* Re-entered service as transport MAGALLANES. *1955:* Sold to Compania Minera Santa Barbara, Chile and renamed SANBAR. *1957:* Broke down at the Panama Canal and subsequently sold to Solmar Cia. Nav.; Panama, being renamed SPRINGWATER. *9.1958:* Sold to Cantieri Navali del Golfo, Spezia for breaking up after lying at that port since *30.4.1958.*

M6. EMPIRE CONVEYOR (1939-1940)
ON.140672. 5,911g, 3,682n. 400.3 x 51.6 x 32.9 feet.
T. 3-cyl. by Blair & Co. Ltd., Stockton.
6.1917: Completed by Richardson, Duck & Co. Ltd., Stockton as FARNWORTH for the Dalgliesh Steam Shipping Co. Ltd. (R. S. Dalgliesh manager), Newcastle. *1924:* Sold to the Harlem S.S. Co. Ltd. (F. Newsom manager), London and renamed ILLINOIS. *1924:* Management taken over by Brown, Jenkinson & Co. *1927:* Sold to Compagnie Générale Transatlantique, France, same name. *1934:* Sold to Rethymnis & Kulukundis Ltd., London. *1934:* Resold to M. Kulukundis (Rethymnis & Kulukundis Ltd. managers), Greece and renamed MOUNT PENTELIKON. *1936:* Owners restyled: Kulukundis Brothers. *1938:* Owners restyled: Kulukundis Shipping Co. S.A. *1939:* Sold to 'Orion' Schiffahrts G.m.b.H. (E. Behnke manager), Germany and renamed GLORIA. *21.10.1939:* Captured S.E. of Iceland by H.M.S. SHEFFIELD. Transferred to Ministry of Shipping. *12.1939:* Placed under Hogarth management. *1940:* Renamed EMPIRE CONVEYOR. *20.6.1940:* Torpedoed and sunk by U.122 about 50 miles South of Barra Head, Hebrides, in position 56.16N. 08.10W. Captain F. B. MacIntyre was killed.

M7. EMPIRE PROGRESS (1940-1942)
ON.142320. 5,249g, 3,204n. 400.6 x 52.3 x 28.5 feet.
T. 3-cyl. by D. Rowan & Co. Ltd., Glasgow.
3.1918: Completed by Harland & Wolff Ltd., Glasgow as the tank steamer WAR EXPERT for The Shipping Controller (Anglo-Saxon Petroleum Co. Ltd. managers). *1919:* Purchased by the Anglo-Saxon Petroleum Co. Ltd., London and renamed ANOMIA. *1927:* Sold to Akties. Brovigseil (Th. Brovig manager), Norway and renamed ANDREA. *1938:* Sold to M. Querci, Italy and renamed MUGNONE. Converted into a dry cargo ship. *6.1940:* Seized at Newcastle-on-Tyne. Taken over by the Ministry of Shipping (later Ministry of War Transport) and renamed EMPIRE PROGRESS. Placed under Hogarth management. *22.5.1941:* Bombed and gunned by aircraft 3 miles S.W. of the Needles. *13.4.1942:* Torpedoed and sunk by U.402 in the North Atlantic, South of Cape Race, in position 40.29N. 52.35W. while on a voyage from Glasgow to Tampa, Fla. Captain T. S. Hewitt and 10 crew members killed and two wounded.

M8. TYSA (1940-1942)
5,327g, 3,179n. 434.1 x 59.3 x 24.1 feet.
7-cyl. 2 S.C.S.A. oil engine by the Shipbuilders.
12.1938: Completed by N.V. Machinefabriek en Scheepswerf van P. Smit Jr., Rotterdam for N.V. Maatschappij Vrachtvaart, Holland. *6.1940:* Placed under Hogarth management. *29.6.1942:* Torpedoed by the Italian submarine MOROSINI about 800 miles S.E. of Bermuda, in position 25.30N., 57.49W., whilst on passage from Cape Town to Baltimore. *30.6.1942:* Sunk by gunfire from escorting warships.

M9. YSELHAVEN (1940-1941)
4,802g, 2,987n. 360.0 x 52.0 x 31.5 feet.
T. 3-cyl. by North Eastern Marine Engineering Co. Ltd., Newcastle.
1.1921: Completed by William Dobson & Co., Newcastle for Gebr. Van Uden, Holland. *1925:* Owners restyled: N.V. Gebr. Van Uden's Scheepvaart en Agentuur Maatschappij. *6.1940:* Placed under Hogarth management. *6.6.1941:* Torpedoed and sunk by U.43 in position 49.25N. 40.54W., after convoy OB328 had dispersed, whilst on passage from Liverpool to St. Lawrence River. 24 of her crew were lost.

M10. HAULERWIJK (1940-1941)
3,278g, 1,951n. 325.0 x 48.2 x 23.7 feet.
T. 3-cyl. by the Shipbuilders.
8.1924: Completed by the Clyde Shipbuilding & Engineering Co. Ltd., Port Glasgow for N.V. Stoomschip Maatschappij Noordwijk (Erhardt & Dekkers managers), Holland. *1933:* Registered under N.V. Stoomvaart Maatschappij 'Oisterwijk' under same management. *7.1940:* Placed under Hogarth management. *30.9.1941:* Torpedoed and sunk by U.32 about 1200 miles West of Valentia, Ireland, in position 53.34N. 27.28W., whilst on passage from Milford Haven to Tampa, Fla.

M11. ANADYR (1940-1944)
ON.160888. 5,277g, 3,177n. 412.7 x 55.1 x 26.4 feet.
Q. 4-cyl. by North Eastern Marine Engineering Co. Ltd., Newcastle.
4.1930: Completed by Northumberland Shipbuilding Co. (1927) Ltd., Newcastle as REDSEA for the Sea S.S. Co. Ltd. (Wm. Brown, Atkinson & Co. Ltd. managers), Hull. *1938:* Sold to Cie. des Messageries Maritimes, France and renamed ANADYR. *6.1940:* Taken over by the Ministry of Shipping (later Ministry of War Transport) at Gibraltar. *7.1940:* Placed under Hogarth management. *6.5.1944:* Torpedoed and sunk by U.129 about 600 miles S.S.E. of Recife, Brazil, in position 10.55S. 27.30W. while on a voyage from Trinidad to Table Bay.

M12. S.N.A. 8. (1940-1946)
ON.165977. 2,569g, 1,543n. 296.2 x 45.0 x 20.1 feet.
T. 3-cyl. by the Shipbuilders.
6.1930: Completed by Smith's Dock Co. Ltd., Stockton for Société Nationale d'Affrètements, France. *1940:* Taken over by the Ministry of Shipping (later Ministry of War Transport). *8.1940:* Placed under Hogarth management, and spent the entire period under Hogarth management on the English East Coast, mainly carrying coal from the N.E. Coast to the Thames. *6.1946:* Returned to her French owners. *1960:* Broken up at Toulon by Etablissements Serra Frères.

M13. PRINCE DE LIEGE (1940-1944)
2,588g, 1,332n. 307.4 x 45.2 x 16.8 feet.
6-cyl. 2 S.C.S.A. oil engine by Soc. Anon. John Cockerill, Seraing.
1938: Completed by Soc. Anon. John Cockerill, Hoboken for Cie. 'Dens-Océan' Soc. Anon., Belgium. *8.1940:* Placed under Hogarth management. *10.5.1944:* Hogarth management ceased and vessel returned to the control of her owners. *11.3.1956:* Caught fire off Calaburras Point, Malaga, whilst on passage from Sfax to Granton with esparto grass and phosphates, and abandoned by her

crew. Taken in tow by the Spanish naval tug R.A. 2 and the salvage vessel HERAKLES and *14.3.1956* arrived at Gibraltar and beached. *7.5.1956:* Declared a constructive total loss. *8.1957:* Sold to Italian owners at Trieste and renamed ELAINE MARIA. *6.10.1957:* Left Gibraltar in tow for Trieste where she went to the Arsenale Triestino for repair. It was found, however, that she was beyond economical repair and, by *12.1958,* she had been broken up by the Soc. Industriale Demolizioni Riparazioni Marittime (S.I.D.E.M.A.R.).

M14. EMPIRE MALLARD (1940-1941)
ON168162. 4,957g, 3,475n. 381.4 x 53.2 x 27.0 feet.
T. 3-cyl. by Seattle Construction & Dry Dock Co., Seattle.
9.1918: Completed by Todd Dry Dock & Construction Corp., Tacoma, Wash, as ANACORTES for the United States Shipping Board. *1937:* Taken over by the United States Maritime Commission. *1940:* Sold to Ministry of Shipping. *10.1940:* Placed under Hogarth management. *1941:* Renamed EMPIRE MALLARD. *2.1941:* Taken over at Norfolk, Va. *26.9.1941:* Sank in Belle Isle Strait N.S. after being in collision with EMPIRE MOON whilst on passage from New York to Liverpool.

M15. WESTERN CHIEF (1940-1941)
5,759g, 3,505n. 409.8 x 54.2 x 27.7 feet.
Double reduction geared steam turbines by General Electric Co., Schenectady, N.Y.
7.1918: Completed by Northwest Steel Co., Portland O. for the United States Shipping Board. *1937:* Taken over by the United States Maritime Commission. *10.1940:* Purchased by the Ministry of Shipping and placed under Hogarth Management. *14.3.1941:* Torpedoed and sunk by the Italian submarine EMO about 600 miles South of Reykjavik, in position 58.52N. 21.13W., whilst on her delivery voyage from New York to Newport, Mon. 24 crew killed.

M16. EMPIRE MARINER (1941-1946)
ON.167412. 4,957g, 2,926n. 401.6 x 54.4 x 27.4 feet.
2 steam turbines by Allgemeine Electricitaets Ges., Berlin. *1943:* Re-engined with T. 3-cyl. by Duncan Stewart & Co. Ltd., Glasgow.
1922: Completed by Deutsche Werft A.G., Hamburg as SCHWARZWALD for Hamburg-Amerikanische Packetfahrt Actien-Gesellschaft (Hamburg-Amerika Linie), Germany. *1935:* Sold to H. Vogemann, Germany and renamed RHEINGOLD. *25.10.1939:* Captured in the North Atlantic by H.M.S. DELHI. Transferred to Ministry of Shipping (later Ministry of War Transport). *1940:* Renamed EMPIRE MARINER. *1.1941:* Placed under Hogarth management. *1943:* Re-engined and re-boilered. *12.7.1946:* Sold to the South American Saint Line Ltd. (B. & S. Shipping Co. Ltd. managers), Cardiff and renamed ST.INA. *1948:* Sold to the Bristol City Line of Steamships Ltd. (Chas. Hill & Sons managers), Bristol and renamed WELLS CITY. *1951:* Sold to East & West S.S. Co., Karachi and renamed FAUSTA. *1963:* Sold to Carstairs & Cumming Ltd., Karachi for breaking up. *16.10.1963:* Demolition commenced.

M17. PICOTEE (1941-1947)
ON.133217. 4,307g, 2,725n. 369.9 x 51.1 x 26.1 feet.
T. 3-cyl. by the Shipbuilders.
5.1913: Completed by John Readhead & Sons Ltd., South Shields as TREVIDER for the Hain Steamship Co. Ltd. (Edward Hain & Son managers), St. Ives. *1914:* Detained by Germany at Brake. *1918:* Returned to her owners. *1925:* Managers restyled: Foster, Hain & Read Ltd. *1933:* Sold to 'Ilirija' Navigation Co. Ltd. (Ant. Topic manager), Yugoslavia and renamed ROSINA TOPIC. *1941:* Taken over by the Ministry of Shipping (later Ministry of War Transport) and renamed PICOTEE. *28.2.1941:* Placed under Hogarth management. *1946:* Ostensibly (according to "Lloyd's Register") renamed ROSINA TOPIC and returned to Brodarsko Akcionarsko Drustvo "Oceania", Yugoslavia and later that year renamed LIKA. However she did, in fact, remain as PICOTEE under Hogarth management until *7.8.1947* when she was handed over at London to State Enterprise Jadranska Slobodna Plovidba (Adriatic Tramp Shipping), Yugoslavia and renamed LIKA. *3.1953:* Dismantled at Split, Yugoslavia by Brodospas.

M18. EMPIRE MALLORY (1941-1943)
ON.168684. 6,327g, 4,592n. 407.0 x 54.7 x 33.2 feet.
T. 3-cyl. by D. Rowan & Co. Ltd., Glasgow.
28.8.1941: Completed by C. Connell & Co. Ltd., Glasgow for the Ministry of War Transport and placed under Hogarth Management. *29.1.1943:* Management transferred to Charles Cravos & Co., Cardiff. *1946:* Sold to Ampleforth S.S. Co. Ltd. (Charles Cravos & Co. managers), Cardiff and renamed AMPLEFORTH. *23.1.1947:* Stranded near Tel Aviv after her anchors had dragged, whilst on passage from Cardiff to Haifa and Alexandria. *3.3.1947:* Refloated and arrived at Alexandria where she was abandoned as a constructive total loss. *1947:* Purchased by Irish Bay Lines Ltd. (Henry P. Lenaghan, manager), Belfast, repaired and re-entered service as BANGOR BAY. Managers later restyled: Henry P. Lenaghan & Sons Ltd. *1954:* Sold to the Great Eastern Shipping Co. Ltd., Bombay and renamed JAG SHANTI. *9.9.1961:* Arrived at Bombay for breaking up by Jagatjit Industrial Corporation.

M19. SUPETAR (1941-1942)

ON.127445. 3,748g, 2,373n. 346.4 x 50.8 x 23.1 feet.
T. 3-cyl. by Central Marine Engine Works, West Hartlepool.
1909: Completed by William Gray & Co. Ltd., West Hartlepool as CATERINO for the Gulf Line Ltd.
(Furness, Withy & Co. Ltd. managers), West Hartlepool. *1921:* Sold to N. P. Roussos & Co., Greece
and renamed MARIA N. ROUSSOS. *1932:* Sold to Mme. Marie & K. E. Venizelos, Greece. *1935:*
Sold to Frano Petrinovic, Yugoslavia and renamed SUPETAR. *9.1941:* Taken over by the Ministry of
War Transport and placed under Hogarth management at Calcutta. *13.6.1942:* Torpedoed and sunk
by the Japanese submarine I-16 North of Inhambane, East Africa, in position 21.49S, 35.50E.

M20. THEMISTO (1941-1945)

4,707g, 2,824n. 400.5 x 55.3 x 25.1 feet.
C. 4-cyl. by the Shipbuilders.
1928: Completed by Rotterdamsche Droogdok Maatschappij, Schiedam for N.V. Maatschappij
Zeevaart (Hudig & Veder managers), Holland. *20.9.1941:* Placed under Hogarth management at
Liverpool. *4.7.1945:* Returned to her Dutch owners. *1958:* Sold to Compania Maritima di Isola
Spetsai, Costa Rica and renamed SPETSAI NAVIGATOR. *1962:* Registered under the Panamanian
flag by her owners and renamed NAVIGATOR. *1963:* Sold to Brodospas, Split for breaking up.
9.1963: Demolition commenced.

M21. OMBILIN (1942)

5,658g, 3,195n. 420.4 x 54.2 x 24.3 feet.
T. 3-cyl. by Nederlandsche Fabriek van Werktuigen & Spoorweg-Materieel, Amsterdam.
1915: Completed by Nederlandsche Scheepsbouw Maatschappij, Amsterdam for the Koninklijke
Paketvaart Maatschappij, Amsterdam. *3.1942:* Placed under Hogarth management. *12.12.1942:*
Torpedoed and sunk by the Italian submarine ENRICO TAZZOLI N.W. of Ceara, Brazil, in position
07.30N. 39.30W., whilst on passage from Trinidad to Cape Town.

M22. PIETER DE HOOGH (1942-1945)

ON.169001. 7,168g, 4,290n. 423.8 x 57.2 x 34.9 feet.
T. 3-cyl. by North Eastern Marine Engineering Co. (1938) Ltd., Sunderland.
12.1941: Completed by Joseph L. Thompson & Sons Ltd., Sunderland as EMPIRE HALLEY for the
Ministry of War Transport (W. T. Gould & Co. managers). *1942:* Transferred to the Netherlands
Shipping & Trading Committee Ltd., renamed PIETER DE HOOGH and placed under management of
Escombe, McGrath & Co. *3.1942:* Placed under Hogarth management at Hull. *16.6.1945:*
Management transferred to Escombe, McGrath & Co. *6.1945:* Management taken over by N.V. Van
Nievelt Goudriaan & Co.'s Stoomvaart Maatschappij. *1947:* Sold to N.V. Stoomvaart Maatschappij
Oostzee (Vinke & Co., later Vinke & Zonen, managers), Holland and renamed BRITSUM. *1959:* Sold
to the Marubeni-Iida Co. Ltd., Tokyo. *24.8.1959:* Arrived at Osaka for breaking up by the Kitagawa
Sangyo K.K.

M23. OCEAN VOYAGER (1942-1943)

ON.168831. 7.174g, 4,274n. 425.1 x 57.0 x 34.8 feet.
T. 3-cyl. by General Machinery Corp., Hamilton, Ohio.
4.1942: Completed by Todd California S. B. Corp., Richmond, Cal. for the Ministry of War
Transport and placed under Hogarth management. *19.3.1943:* Bombed in Tripoli Harbour. Sank the
following day. Captain D. MacKellar and 4 crew killed and a further 10 wounded.

M24. FORT CHILCOTIN (1942-1943)

ON.168318. 7,133g, 4,257n. 424.6 x 57.2 x 34.9 feet.
T. 3-cyl. by Dominion Engineering Works Ltd., Montreal.
6.6.1942: Completed by West Coast Shipbuilders Ltd., Vancouver, B.C. for the United States War
Shipping Administration and bareboat-chartered to the Ministry of War Transport. Placed under
Hogarth management. *24.7.1943:* Torpedoed and sunk by U.172 about 750 miles South of Recife,
Brazil, in position 15.03S. 32.35W., with the loss of 4 crew.

M25. FORT PITT (1942-1948)

ON.168738. 7,133g, 4,257n. 424.6 x 57.2 x 34.9 feet.
T. 3-cyl. by Dominion Engineering Works Ltd., Montreal.
28.7.1942: Completed by Burrard Dry Dock Co. Ltd., N. Vancouver, B.C. for the United States War
Shipping Administration and bareboat-chartered to the Ministry of War Transport. Placed under
Hogarth management. *17.1.1948:* Returned to United States Maritime Commission. *20.3.1959:*
Arrived at Mobile for breaking up by Pinto Island Metals Co. on behalf of Commercial Metals Co.,
Dallas.

OCEAN VANQUISHER *Builder's photograph*

M26. OCEAN VANQUISHER (1942)

ON.167134. 7,174g, 4,272n. 425.1 x 57.0 x 34.8 feet.
T. 3-cyl. by General Machinery Corp., Hamilton, O.
7.1942: Completed by Permanente Metals Corp. (Shipyard No. 1), Richmond, Cal. for the Ministry of War Transport and placed under Hogarth management. *12.12.1942:* Sunk by Italian frogmen from the Submarine AMBRA using a limpet mine N.W. of Algiers, in position 36.48N. 03.04E., with the loss of two crew. *8.1.1943:* Declared a constructive total loss. *27.7.1945:* Arrived at Oran for temporary repairs and sailed for Palermo where she arrived *6.2.1946.* By *9.1946* Sold to the Cantieri Navali Riuniti, Italy rebuilt and resold by them to the Societa Ligure di Armamento, Italy who renamed her NEREO. *13.11.1963:* Arrived at Hirao, Japan for breaking up by the Matsukura Co. Ltd.

M27. FORT ASSINIBOINE (1943-1946)

ON.168480. 7,128g, 4,248n. 424.6 x 57.2 x 34.9 feet.
T. 3-cyl. by Dominion Engineering Works Ltd., Montreal.
28.4.1943: Completed by Burrard Dry Dock Co. Ltd., N. Vancouver, B.C. for the Dominion of Canada and bareboat-chartered to the Ministry of War Transport. Placed under Hogarth management. *27.4.1946:* Management transfered to Wm. Brown, Atkinson & Co. Ltd., Hull. *1948:* Sold to the Laurentian S.S. Co. Ltd., Montreal and renamed LAURENTIAN LAKE. Shortly afterwards transferred to Laurentian Overseas Shipping Ltd. *1950:* Re-registered in London and placed under the management of Coulouthros Ltd. *1951:* Management transferred to Fern Hill S.S. Co. Ltd. *1954:* Sold to Monovar Cia. Nav. S.A., Liberia and renamed OLYMPOS. *1960:* Sold to Cia. de Nav. Cerra Guaca S.A., Greece and renamed PENTELI II. *1963:* Sold to Corona Cia. Nav., Greece and renamed GIALIA. *1963:* Sold to Marimperio Cia. Nav. S.A., Greece and renamed PAXOI. *14.3.1967:* Sailed from Singapore for a Chinese mainland port for breaking up.

M28. SRBIN (1943-1945)

982g, 602n. 215.7 x 30.6 x 14.0 feet.
T. 3-cyl. by the Shipbuilders.
8.1913: Completed by Hall, Russell & Co. Ltd., Aberdeen as SPARTA for the Società in Azioni Ungaro Croata di Nav. Marittima a Vap., Austria-Hungary. *1921:* Allocated as a prize to Jugoslavia. *1922:* Sold to Jadranska Plovitba Soc. in Azioni di Nav., Jugoslavia and renamed SRBIN. *1926:* Owners restyled: Jadranska Plovidba D.D. *1941:* Seized by Italy and renamed CARLO BORSINI. *10.1943:* Recovered and placed under Hogarth management. *31.5.1945:* Returned to her Jugoslavian owners at Naples. *1947:* Taken over by State Enterprise Jadranska Linijska Plovidba (Adriatic Line). *6.6.1947:* Sunk by mine off Glavotok Point, Veglia Island, whilst on passage from Split to Rijeka. Refloated and condemned as a total loss.

M29. EMPIRE DUKE (1943-1945)
ON.180048. 7,240g, 4,179n. 432.8 x 57.2 x 35.9 feet.
T. 3-cyl. by Duncan Stewart & Co. Ltd., Glasgow.
30.11.1943: Completed by Joseph L. Thompson & Sons Ltd., Sunderland for the Ministry of War Transport and placed under Hogarth management. *6.1944:* Took part in the Normandy Landings. *5.1945:* Sold to the French Government (Ministère de la Marine Marchande) and renamed LIEUTENANT J. LE MEUR. Placed under management of Compagnie Générale Transatlantique. *1949:* Sold to Cie. Franco-Chérifienne de Nav., Morocco and renamed ZELIDJA. *1955:* Sold to the Cia. de Nav. Hellespont S.A., Liberia and renamed PROPONTIS. *1957:* Sold to Cia. de Nav. Propontis, Liberia, same name. *1962:* Transferred to Greek registry. *1966:* Sold to Formosan shipbreakers. *24.5.1966:* Arrived at Kaohsiung for breaking up.

EMPIRE PLOUGHMAN as 'Baron Geddes'   *J. H. Cleet*

M30. EMPIRE PLOUGHMAN See BARON GEDDES (No. 125).

M31. EMPIRE RANSOM See BARON ELIBANK (No. 127).

M32. EMPIRE DUCHESS (1943-1946)
ON.180051. 7,067g, 4,879n. 431.0 x 56.3 x 35.2 feet.
T. 3-cyl. by J. Dickinson & Sons Ltd., Sunderland.
13.12.1943: Completed by Short Bros. Ltd., Sunderland for the Ministry of War Transport and placed under Hogarth management. *7.8.1946:* Management transferred to the Union-Castle Mail Steamship Co. Ltd. *1949:* Purchased by the Union-Castle Mail Steamship Co. Ltd. and renamed BRAEMAR CASTLE. *1950:* Sold to King Line Ltd., London and renamed KING JAMES. *1958:* Sold to Cambay Prince S.S. Co. Ltd. (John Manners & Co. Ltd. managers), Hong Kong and renamed TYNE BREEZE. *1963:* Sold to the Cathay Trader Steamship Co. Ltd., Hong Kong and renamed CATHAY TRADER. *1964:* Sold to the Pacific Pearl Nav. Co. Ltd., Hong Kong and renamed PEARL LIGHT. *1966:* Sold to the Marikar Navigation & Agencies Ltd., Hong Kong and renamed HABIB MARIKAR. *3.11.1967:* Suffered an engine breakdown whilst on passage from Hong Kong to Chittagong and later grounded on Lincoln Island, in position 16.30N. 112.50E., becoming a total loss.

M33. FORT ST. ANTOINE (1943-1946)
ON.169985. 7,165g 4,237n. 424.6 x 57.2 x 34.9 feet.
T. 3-cyl. by The John Inglis Co. Ltd., Toronto, Ont.
17.12.1943: Completed by North Van Ship Repairs Ltd., N. Vancouver, B.C. for the Dominion of Canada and bareboat-chartered to the Ministry of War Transport. Placed under Hogarth management. *30.7.1946:* Returned to the Canadian Government and managed for them by the Park

S.S. Co. Ltd. *1947:* Sold to Kerr Silver Lines (Canada) Ltd., Vancouver and renamed MANX FISHER. *1949:* Sold to Muhammadi S.S. Co. Ltd., Karachi and renamed AL HASAN. *5.1963:* Severely damaged at Chittagong by collision and grounding due to a cyclone. *1964:* Sold to Pakistan shipbreakers. *6.2.1964:* Arrived at Karachi for breaking up by Haji Yousuf Ismail Mala & Co. *17.2.1964:* Demolition commenced.

EMPIRE HARCOURT as 'Baron Ailsa'   *J. H. Cleet*

M34. EMPIRE HARCOURT See BARON AILSA (No. 128)

M35. SAMBANKA (1944-1947)
ON.180032. 7,219g, 4,380n. 422.8 x 57.0 x 34.8 feet.
T. 3-cyl. by Springfield Machine & Foundry Co., Springfield, Mass.
22.4.1944: Completed by the New England S. B. Corp., Portland, Me. for the United States War Shipping Administration and bareboat-chartered to the Ministry of War Transport. Placed under Hogarth management. *21.8.1947:* Returned to the United States Maritime Commission and later taken over by the U.S. Dept. of Commerce. *9.3.1966:* Sold to the Northern Metal Co., Philadelphia for 'Non-transportation use'. *1.1967:* Demolition began at Philadelphia.

M36. EMPIRE NEWFOUNDLAND (1944-1946)
ON.180076. 3,539g, 2,257n. 315.5 x 46.5 x 22.1 feet.
T. 3-cyl. by Central Marine Engine Works (Wm. Gray & Co. Ltd.), West Hartlepool.
5.9.1944: Completed by William Gray & Co. Ltd., West Hartlepool for the Ministry of War Transport and placed under Hogarth management. *31.8.1946:* Management transferred to H. P. Lenaghan, later H. P. Lenaghan & Sons Ltd., Belfast. *1949:* Purchased by Irish Bay Lines Ltd. (H. P. Lenaghan & Sons Ltd. managers) Belfast and later the same year sold to F. T. Everard & Sons Ltd., London and renamed ETHEL EVERARD. *1954:* Sold to the Indo-China Steam Navigation Co. Ltd., Hong Kong and renamed HOP SANG. *1962:* Renamed HANG SANG, same owners. *1968:* Sold to the Fui Nam Co. Ltd., Hong Kong and renamed HOI SOON. *1969:* Sold to Chan Cheung Man (Fui Nam Co. Ltd. managers), Somali Republic. *12.3.1970:* Delivered to Yuen Hing Godown Co., who began demolition at Hong Kong *15.3.1970.*

M37.EMPIRE CANNING (1945-1946)
ON.166219. 6,997g, 4,934n. 427.1 x 56.3 x 35.2 feet.
8-cyl. 4 S.C S.A. oil engine by Hawthorn, Leslie & Co. Ltd., Newcastle.
1944: Completed by the Caledon Shipbuilding & Engineering Co. Ltd., Dundee for the Ministry of War Transport and, in *1.1945,* placed under Hogarth management. *6.6.1946:* Sold to the Britain S.S. Co. Ltd. (Watts, Watts & Co. Ltd. managers), London and renamed WILLESDEN. *1958:* Sold to Lambda Shipping Co. Ltd. (World-Wide Co. (Shipping Managers) Ltd. managers), Hong Kong and renamed GOLDEN LAMBDA. *1960:* Sold to the Neptune Shipping Co. Ltd., Hong Kong and renamed MARINE EXPLORER. *1962:* Sold to Viking Shipping Co. Ltd., Hong Kong and renamed EAST VIM. *1963:* Renamed WAKASA BAY, same owners. *1966:* Sold to Leo Shipping Co. Ltd. (World-Wide (Shipping) Ltd. managers), Hong Kong and renamed GOLDEN WIND. *16.11.1966:* Arrived at Wakayama for breaking up by Mitsui & Co. Ltd. *8.12.1966:* Demolition began at Tsuneishi-cho, Hiroshima.

M38. EMPIRE CAICOS (1945-1946)

ON.180082. 3,538g, 2,259n. 315.5 x 46.5 x 22.1 feet.
T. 3-cyl. by Central Marine Engine Works (Wm. Gray & Co. Ltd.), West Hartlepool.
5.1945: Completed by William Gray & Co. Ltd., West Hartlepool for the Ministry of War Transport and placed under Hogarth management. *12.10.1946:* Management taken over by the Rodney Steamship Co. Ltd., London. *1950:* Sold to Silvertown Services Ltd., London, renamed SUGAR TRANSPORTER and placed under the management of R.S. Dalgliesh Ltd., Newcastle. *1951:* Sold to Kentships Ltd. (same managers). *1951:* Resold to Silvertown Services Ltd., under same managers. *1952:* Dalgliesh management terminated. *1956:* Transferred to Silvertown Services Shipping Ltd. *1957:* Sold to James Paterson & Co. Proprietary Ltd., Melbourne and renamed PATTAWILYA. *11.1961:* James Paterson & Co. Pty. Ltd. were taken over by McIlwraith, McEacharn Ltd., Melbourne. *1962:* Sold to the Cronulla Shipping Co. Ltd. (John Manners & Co. Ltd. managers), Hong Kong and renamed CLOVELLY. *1963:* Transferred to the San Jeronimo Steamship Co. S.A., Panama, under the same management. *13.5.1967:* Arrived at Uchiumi, Shodo Island for breaking up by Sanoyasu Shoji K.K., after sustaining heavy weather damage in *1.1967.*

M39. EMPIRE ADEN (1945-1946)

ON.180156. 7,308g, 5,052n. 431.2 x 56.3 x 35.6 feet.
T. 3-cyl. by the North Eastern Marine Engineering Co. (1938) Ltd., Sunderland.
14.5.1945: Completed by Bartram & Sons Ltd., Sunderland for the Ministry of War Transport and placed under Hogarth management. *28.8.1946:* Management transferred at Melbourne to Andrew Weir & Co., Glasgow. *1948:* Purchased by the Bank Line Ltd. (Andrew Weir & Co. Ltd., later the Andrew Weir Shipping & Trading Co. Ltd., managers), Glasgow and renamed ETIVEBANK. *1955:* Sold to the Alcyone Shipping Co. Ltd., London and renamed ALCYONE FORTUNE. *1958:* Sold to the Pan Norse S.S. Co. S.A., Panama and renamed NORTHERN VENTURE. *1966:* Wah Kwong & Co. (Hong Kong) Ltd. became managers. *9.6.1967:* Went aground off Adaga Shima, Okinawa, in a position 26.45N. 128.21E., whilst on passage from Tsukumi to Manila, and was abandoned by her crew.

M40. BANFF PARK (1945-1947)

ON.173264. 7,133g, 4,258n. 424.6 x 57.2 x 34.9 feet.
T. 3-cyl. by the Dominion Engineering Works Ltd., Montreal.
9.1942: Completed by Davie Shipbuilding & Repairing Co. Ltd., Lauzon P.Q. for the Dominion of Canada and placed under management of the Park S.S. Co. Ltd. *8.1945:* Bareboat-chartered to the Ministry of War Transport and placed under Hogarth management at Quebec. *4.3.1947:* Management transferred to the Ohlson S.S. Co. Ltd., Hull. *1949:* Management transferred to the Joseph Constantine S.S. Line Ltd., Middlesbrough. *1950:* Sold to the Rex Shipping Co. Ltd. (Hadjilias & Co. Ltd. managers), London and renamed OAKHURST. *1957:* Sold to the Asturias Shipping Co. S.A., Liberia and renamed CATALUNIA. *1958:* Sold to the Grenehurst Shipping Co. Ltd., London, same name. *1961:* Sold to Valia Compania Naviera S.A., Greece and renamed XENOPHON. *26.10.1962:* Went aground near Les Pierres Noires, Ushant, whilst on passage from Cardiff to Venice with coal, and was abandoned by her crew.

M41. EMPIRE CALSHOT (1945-1946)

ON.180352. 7,133g, 4,934n. 427.1 x 57.0 x 35.4 feet.
3-cyl. 2 S.C.S.A. oil engine by William Doxford & Sons Ltd., Sunderland.
11.1945: Completed by the Burntisland Shipbuilding Co. Ltd., Burntisland for the Ministry of War Transport and placed under Hogarth management. *22.3.1946:* Sold to McCowen & Gross Ltd., London and renamed DERRYCUNIHY. *1952:* Sold to the Argobeam Shipping Co. Ltd. (A. Lusi Ltd. managers), London and renamed ARGOBEAM. *1955:* Sold to the Turnbull Scott Shipping Co. Ltd. (Turnbull, Scott & Co. managers), London and renamed PARKGATE. *1961:* Sold to Patlem Compania Naviera S.A., Lebanon and renamed PANAGOS. *1968:* Sold to Chinese mainland shipbreakers. *29.9.1968:* Arrived at Shanghai for breaking up.

M42. EMPIRE TERN (1946)

ON.167594. 2,479g, 1,502n. 251.0 x 43.6 x 26.1 feet.
T. 3-cyl. by the Shipbuilders, at Detroit.
12.1919: Completed by the Detroit S. B. Co., Wyandotte as LAKE INGLENOOK for the United States Shipping Board. *1927:* Sold to the New England, New York & Texas S. S. Corp., U.S.A. *1928:* Sold to the Newton S. S. Corp., U.S.A. *1932:* Renamed TEXAS BANKER, same owners. *1940:* Purchased by the Ministry of Shipping (later Ministry of War Transport), London and renamed EMPIRE TERN. Placed under the management of Sir William Reardon Smith & Sons Ltd., Cardiff. *8.5.1946:* Placed under Hogarth management while lying at Hull. *1946:* Sold to Williamson & Co., Hong Kong being transferred at Hull 29.7.1946. *1949:* Renamed INCHMULL by her owners and registered under the Inchmull S. S. Co. Ltd. *1953:* Sold to the Sigma Shipping Co. Ltd., Hong Kong and renamed SIGMA STAR. *16.10.1953:* Arrived at Osaka for breaking up.

INDEX

ACKNOWLEDGEMENTS

For their help in the preparation of this history we are indebted to Messrs. Somner and Chesterton of the World Ship Society Central Record Team, Messrs. Littlejohn and Pryde of Lloyds Register of Shipping, Mr. R. H. Gibson of Grasmere. Mr. R. M. Hackman, Mr. R. R. Y. N. Malo, Mr. R. J. M. Robinson and Dr. W. Marshall Walker.
The Society also gratefully acknowledges the encouragement of the late Mr. Hugh Hogarth.
Photographs where not otherwise acknowledged are from the archives of H. Hogarth & Sons, Ltd.